Therapy Online

Also by Kate Anthony:

Technology in Counselling and Psychotherapy: A Practitioner's Guide
(edited with Stephen Goss)

The Authors:

DeeAnna Merz Nagel and **Kate Anthony** are both former Presidents of the International Society for Mental Health Online (ISMHO). The combination of their experience presents a breadth of knowledge about online counseling and supervision, encompassing publications, presentations at international, national, regional and state conferences, consultation with many organizations, teaching and facilitating online counselling and supervision, and participating in international, national, regional and local organizations.

Kate Anthony, MSc, FBACP is a psychotherapist, consultant and international expert regarding online counseling and the impact of technology on mental health. She runs OnlineCounsellors.co.uk, a training company for mental health practitioners who wish to work with clients online, and is joint-CEO with DeeAnna of the Online Therapy Institute. She is a published expert on such topics as the use of email, bulletin boards, IRC, videoconferencing, stand-alone software and more radical innovative use of technology within therapeutic practice, such as virtual reality. She co-authored the 1st, 2nd and 3rd editions of the BACP *Guidelines for Online Counselling and Psychotherapy* (*Including Guidelines for Online Supervision*). She presents internationally at conferences and is co-editor of *Technology in Counselling and Psychotherapy: A Practitioner's Guide* (2003). Kate was awarded Fellowship of the British Association for Counselling and Psychotherapy in 2008.

DeeAnna Merz Nagel, LPC, DCC is a psychotherapist, consultant and international expert regarding online counseling and the impact of technology on mental health. She specializes in text-based counseling and supervision via chat and email. DeeAnna's expertise extends to assisting individuals and families in understanding the impact of technology in their lives, from normalizing the use of technology and social media to overcoming Internet and cybersex addictions. Her presentations and publications include ethical considerations for the mental health practitioner with regard to online counseling, social networking, mixed reality and virtual world environments.

Therapy Online

A Practical Guide

Kate Anthony
and
DeeAnna Merz Nagel

Los Angeles | London | New Delhi
Singapore | Washington DC

SAGE Publications Ltd
1 Oliver's Yard
55 City Road
London EC1Y 1SP

SAGE Publications Inc.
2455 Teller Road
Thousand Oaks, California 91320

SAGE Publications India Pvt Ltd
B 1/I 1 Mohan Cooperative Industrial Area
Mathura Road
New Delhi 110 044

SAGE Publications Asia-Pacific Pte Ltd
33 Pekin Street #02-01
Far East Square
Singapore 048763

Library of Congress Control Number: 2009927112

British Library Cataloguing in Publication data

A catalogue record for this book is available from the British Library

ISBN 978-1-84920-473-6

Typeset by C&M Digitals Pvt Ltd, Chennai, India
Printed in Great Britain by TJ International Ltd, Padstow, Cornwall
Printed on paper from sustainable resources

Mixed Sources
Product group from well-managed forests and other controlled sources
www.fsc.org Cert no. SGS-COC-2482
© 1996 Forest Stewardship Council
FSC

To P – one and the same in our own different way ^_^, my godson Jamie (it's your turn, lol), and in loving memory of my father Nick Bartlett, sorely missed :o(

To Pete – my constant, to ma & pa – my foundation, to MJ – my rock. To JA (you know why – waaaay back to now) and to my goddaughter Savannah – young but wise soul [smiling] … btw S – your mama thinks you & I are alike in some ways … :)

And finally to the critters – Bikkit, Bunky, Tula, Reva, Licky and Allsorts … (Reva says 'Friend Me' via Catbook app on Facebook!)

CONTENTS

FOREWORD

In the mid 1990s, I was part of a counseling service that offered 'Phone Counseling'. I selected a schedule of times I would be available by phone for individuals calling into the service for a counseling session. The sessions were conducted over the phone. The client called in on a '976' line and gave the operator his or her credit card number. The call was then transferred to my phone number and I did 'phone counseling'. The client was charged by the minute.

While telephone counseling had been around for 35 years, for our service, there were legal and ethical issues that cropped up that had not been considered. That, and the fact that the '976' lines were sometimes used by psychics and escort services, gave it a less than ideal reputation. The service closed only months after it started.

Here we are – just 15 years later. This is a fascinating time for mental health practitioners around the world. Everyone from four-year-olds to seniors uses the Internet. This means potential clients in the general population are becoming more sophisticated in regard to seeking emotional or relationship help. They research their symptoms on the Internet and learn about DSM diagnoses and a myriad of treatment alternatives.

Further, with the increasing interactivity of the Internet there is an expectation of instant connection and services rendered. People can 'twitter' a question and get an immediate response from a myriad of experts and non-experts on social networking sites. This desire for and expectation of instantaneous response in our day-to-day communications leads potential therapy clients to expect the same when it comes to mental health treatment. Many would like to connect to a therapist quickly and participate in therapy in a way that serves them and their schedule. Increasingly, the time taken to travel to and from a therapist's office for a face-to-face session is viewed as an extraordinary waste of time.

As a profession, we must respond to the global socio-cultural changes in our client base if we are to survive. For years, we have challenged existing therapeutic theories but until now, we have not changed our delivery model. The culture is asking us to do that now.

The fact that you picked up this book means you know it too.

This is an amazing book. Not only is it filled with interesting history about the Internet and online therapy, Kate Anthony and DeeAnna Merz Nagel have provided a solid roadmap for you to follow as you dip your toe into a new way of delivering psychotherapy services.

You will finish this book with a concrete understanding and a wealth of ideas about:

- The dos and don'ts of online therapy
- The theory that underpins the work
- The ethical considerations of how to decide if a client is a good candidate for online therapy
- How to attract more new clients by offering more technological alternatives to traditional therapy
- How to market your services
- How to seek further training, supervision, and do research online
- How to use technology to enhance the therapeutic experience of your clients
- How to use social networking for professional growth.

   This book is filled with step-by-step instructions, examples and a strong verbatim case study of the whole therapeutic process, from intake to ending. It is a book that you will refer to again and again if you decide to expand the way you currently offer therapy services. Whether you are new to online therapy or are a veteran, there is much to learn from this book.

Online therapy is not just an idea for the future. Its time has come.

I wish you continued success in your journey to make a difference in the lives of others.

Casey Truffo, MFT

CEO and Founder of The Therapist Leadership Institute
and BeaWealthy Therapist.com

ACKNOWLEDGEMENTS

The authors would like to acknowledge the help and support during the development of the book of Stephen Goss, Tom Merz, Casey Truffo, the dedicated team at SAGE, friends, family and the many colleagues in both the online and offline world too numerous to mention, but particularly the members and friends of the Online Therapy Institute.

INTRODUCTION

OVERVIEW OF THE CURRENT TEXT

Welcome to *Therapy Online: A Practical Guide*. The main purpose of this book is to disseminate our practical experience and academic knowledge of working with text online, and enable the reader to learn from our expertise gained in over 10 years in online therapy, from our perspective as two leading experts in the field from either side of the Atlantic. In addition, no textbook on the topic would be complete without wider reference to the use of technology in therapy *without* the use of a keyboard, and we aim to introduce the reader to some of these facets of the work along the way.

We hope this will encourage further reading of the material already written and also emerging as technology develops and is applied to therapy and the mental health field. While we discuss the theory of therapy online, we also discuss the practice and ethics, including a detailed case study to exemplify some of the issues peculiar to working online therapeutically. Therefore, this book is aimed at the practitioner already working online and looking to improve and enhance their service, as well as those considering practicing online in the future or who are undertaking training in therapy and who therefore need to deepen their understanding of the changing profession in light of new technology.

Chapter 1, 'Theoretical Aspects of Online Therapy' discusses online therapy from the point of view of three major theoretical orientations: Humanism, the Psychodynamic school of thought and Cognitive-Behavioral Therapy (CBT). These are discussed within themes common in traditional therapy, such as being an authentic practitioner with a sound level of self-knowledge, and having an understanding of the importance of the therapeutic relationship as underpinning the ability of the client to make changes in his or her life.

Other themes discussed are around empathy, unconditional positive regard, transference and counter-transference, fantasy, and defense mechanisms, as they appear online. We do not mean to suggest that only these theoretical elements are applicable to online work – quite the contrary. By examining theories particular to three main schools of thought, we aim to illustrate for the reader how their own orientation may be thought of in terms of being applicable to online work. Online therapy is a method of delivery, much as Freud's letter writing was – it is what the practitioner brings to the work that counts. The chapter ends with describing a model based on one of the authors' original empirical research.

Chapter 2, 'Essential Skills and Considerations of Online Therapy', examines what is needed to be an effective online therapist, and indeed an effective online client. It discusses how to determine if online therapy is a suitable method of delivery for the practitioner, and how to adapt existing skills to online work, such as being attentive, mirroring the client, summarizing and probing.

Also addressed within this chapter is the consideration needed in communications between practitioner and client *between* contracted sessions, and the importance of encryption for even the most simple housekeeping communications, such as confirming appointment times. Boundaries around this are discussed, with reference to sharing resources, journal-keeping, homework exercises and short 'check-in' emails. The necessary client skills section focuses on determining whether online therapy is suitable for the client from the outset as part of the overall initial intake and assessment process. Suler's (2004) six aspects of disinhibition are looked at by the authors in detail. The chapter ends with example questions that may offer insight into the potential client's ability to work online with the therapist via the intake questionnaire.

Chapter 3, 'Working Without a Physical Presence', gives an in-depth look at how we communicate online without reliance on the physical presence – historically seen as a drawback to online work but increasingly seen also to be one of the benefits. Using examples, we examine appropriate and inappropriate communication via email, and discuss fully the 10 rules of Netiquette as they apply to the mental health field. The chapter then narrows down to focus on the specifics of Netiquette, such as use of emoticons, acronyms and abbreviations, and how to enhance text to convey what is meant by the written message. The conclusion to this chapter identifies the five most likely reasons misunderstandings may occur.

Chapter 4, 'Ethical Considerations', discusses a new global framework for therapy online based on what the authors define as the 'big five' – American (EthicsCode, NBCC, ACA), United Kingdom (BACP) and Cyberspace (ISMHO). These five publications (web-based apart from BACP) comprise guidelines, suggested principles and recommendations for online practice. The chapter discusses the ethical implications when considering informed consent, practitioner competence, client inclusion and client exclusion.

Perhaps most importantly, this chapter introduces a new 'Ethical Framework for the Use of Technology in Mental Health', encompassing several defined and extensive recommendations on practitioners' understanding of the technology, on working within their scope of practice, on seeking out training, knowledge and supervision, on ensuring pertinent and all necessary information is displayed on websites, on the intake and assessment process, and recommendations on informed consent. This global framework is the first of its kind, and draws on the considerable experience of both authors in working with organizations worldwide in developing ethical standards and guidelines.

Chapter 5, 'The Business of Online Therapy', is an extensive analysis on what practitioners really need to know to offer a range of tools for setting up and marketing a practice as well as providing a successful and ethical service. This chapter is of relevance even to the practitioner who has decided that working online is not appropriate in their particular case, as the basics of hosting a simple website to promote and advertise their face-to-face or other services is often overlooked. The chapter draws upon, not only the authors' knowledge, but also that of 'famous names' internationally such as Casey Truffo, who wrote the Foreword to this book. Advice is given on deciding whether joining an e-clinic is desirable, as well as on setting up in private practice as an adjunct or a stand-alone service.

Alongside these considerations are the next steps, for instance what you need to know about an organizational service provider in order to make an informed decision as to their reputation and reliability. Offering a more personalised approach within a private practice means beginning with the basics, such as appointment setting and payment methods, through to the more complex marketing strategies required to be a successful online counselor. The chapter also covers the concept of creating a presence in Second Life which, although seemingly off the beaten path as far as online therapy goes, can actually serve as another extension of a website – a three dimensional advert.

Chapter 6, 'Case Study', is a detailed client case of a woman in her 50s experiencing symptoms of anxiety and depression stemming from an attack she experienced as a young teenager. Designed as an illustration of how an online therapy case could and should be conducted, the chapter guides the reader through Mary's experience from her initial research into finding a therapist, through intake and assessment, email exchanges, SMS contact, necessary because of a technological breakdown, a crisis chat room session, and finally to closure and termination of the contract.

Verbatim transcripts of the therapeutic process between Mary and her therapist Clara guide you through the process of Mary's journey, including her experience of technology in relation to her young teenage daughter's use of it in everyday life. Although fictional, Mary is a composite drawn from the authors' wide experience of online and offline clients and also the use of technology to conduct a therapeutic relationship.

Chapter 7, 'Training Online Therapists', provides an examination of the training available in transferring offline therapy skills to cyberspace. Both online training and offline (face-to-face) training are discussed to educate the reader as to what is available, and so they may make an informed choice as to what further training can or should be undertaken. The training online section defines many different applications that can be utilized to develop and enhance an online course on any topic, before going on to apply these to training online therapists specifically. We particularly focus on the use of role-play in training online, for which there are arguments both for and against.

The chapter also discusses offline, or face-to-face, training, from conference presentations to full two-day workshops. Both the authors have been training practitioners for many years, and so both aspects of their face-to-face training work is analyzed, defining the UK attitude to workshops being used as Continuing Professional Development (CPD) and the need for therapists in the USA to gain Continuing Education (CE) credits. Also discussed is the process for gaining the Distance Credentialed Counselor (DCC™) certification – a national qualification in the United States, which also offers the option of being applicable to practitioners across the globe.

Chapter 8, 'Supervision, Research and Groups/Couples' provides examination of other considerations when working online. The section on supervision considers the use of technology historically before going on to debate what methods of delivery may or may not be appropriate for online work. Supervision via email, forums and listservs, and chat are discussed, underlining one of the themes running throughout the book regarding encryption being essential.

The section on research, written with Dr Stephen Goss, considers the myriad of ways that research can be undertaken online – both qualitatively and quantitatively – from simply looking up an academic paper to full-scale methods of data collection. The ethical considerations inherent in online research are discussed, such as disinhibition skewing results, alongside the many benefits of conducting research online.

The parts related to groups, couples and families examine the different ways of offering multiple participant services online. Couple therapy is a particularly interesting way of working when using technology, whether the participants are in separate locations or in the same room. The family therapy section notes the usefulness of technology in including younger members in the dynamic because of its appeal (and familiarity). Group work takes advantage of diverse geographical populations, particularly with asynchronous methods of communication. The role of the facilitator is examined, with a focus on group conflict resolution and other group dynamics, in cases such as what happens when the group ends.

Chapter 9: 'A Look to The Future and Concluding Thoughts' defines and discusses other types of technology used in therapy. Landline telephone therapy is examined, and also using mobile phones (cellphones) and SMS texting as both a communication tool and as a means of delivering specific applications such as anger diaries. Along a similar theme, Voice over Internet Protocol (VoIP) and videoconferencing have their own benefits and pitfalls. Websites, wikis and podcasting are looked at, alongside other newer technologies in mental health, such as blogging and social/professional networking. Computerized Cognitive Behavioral Therapy (CCBT) is becoming more widely used since the National Institute for Clinical Excellence (NICE) found it successful in the UK. Another newer use of technology is the use of gaming for therapeutic use, particularly in engaging adolescents in therapy. The importance of the rise of avatar therapy and virtual reality environments in mental health is discussed, before the book's concluding thoughts are presented on Web 2.0 and its implications for us as practitioners, for our clients, and for the profession as a whole.

NOTE ON THE SCOPE OF THE TEXT AND THE LANGUAGE USED

The collaboration of authors from both sides of the Atlantic is deliberate. Addressing an audience that is international is appropriate when discussing a topic that provides therapeutic services globally, regardless of geographical limitations. The scope and language of the book has been kept as internationally applicable as possible. However, some language has been chosen for the sake of consistency, such as using 'therapy' to indicate counselling/counseling and psychotherapy, which are also used interchangeably (McLeod, 1994). Also, we have adopted 'therapists' or 'practitioners' in a similar vein, and used the term 'mental health' to indicate that much of the material here is applicable to different tiers of the profession. We aim for the text to be useful to all practitioners, from students of therapy, to qualified therapists, as well as those offering therapeutic services in medical settings, such as psychiatry. Although sometimes the term 'patient' may be applicable to the person seeking therapeutic help, we will use the term 'client' throughout.

The remit of the book is to provide a theoretical, ethical and practical guide to online therapy using text. Therefore, the book concentrates on the use of email, chat and forums, rather than the wider remit of other technological applications, although these are discussed in the final chapter and included where appropriate at other points within the book. The authors recognize, however, that many of the central themes of this book – and especially the themes in Chapter 4, may overlap and be applicable to other technologies. In addition, duplication of some basic information in chapters is deliberate to allow for each chapter to be read in isolation if preferred. Finally, although the book draws on actual cases experienced in conducting online and offline therapy over the last several years, all case material is fictional.

The remainder of this Introduction prepares you further for reading the book. We offer historical background information about the Internet and a summary of key terms you will encounter throughout the book and within your work as an online therapist.

DECIPHERING CYBERSPACE

Since 1991, when the first incarnation of the World Wide Web was completed, the Internet has become a pervasive element of most of the developed world. The recognized creator of the World Wide Web, Tim Berners-Lee (1998), dreamt of 'a common information space in which we communicate by sharing information'. This dream was certainly realized, but it is the development of the Internet since then and indeed the maturation of it as it morphs into Web 2.0 – or even Web 3.0 – that shows us that the presence of cyberspace in our daily lives is unlikely to dissipate or disappear. On the contrary, the use of the Internet has now spread out from use on a personal computer to mobile devices, and is likely to become even more embedded in our personal and professional lives, without us feeling the need to comment, or even noticing. While early use of the term cyberspace involved very technical capabilities such as sensors, signals, connections, transmissions, processors and controllers, the term has now become ubiquitous in describing personal computers, the Internet, information technology and the culture that goes with being part of an online world. Being part of an online world makes one a Netizen (Hauben and Hauben, 1997) – a collision of Internet and citizen – also sometimes called a Cybercitizen or Internaut.

Many textbooks on the subject of online therapy describe accurately the nature of cyberspace being 'virtual' as opposed to 'physical'. That is, living life online – whether by looking for information on the Web, email, chat rooms, social networking, virtual reality environments, gaming, texting and similar – was distinct from the actual business of day-to-day life in the physical world, referred to as Real Life (RL). It is the position of the authors that this is no longer the case – online life exists *as part of* RL for much of the developed world, particularly for those who were born into a world where the Internet and other technologies such as mobile devices were already considered the norm. While pockets of resistance or ignorance may well still exist among some populations (Nagel, 2008), particularly in the mental health field, the merging of cyberspace and RL has already arrived. For clarity, we refer to the actual location of communication as being *online* or *offline*.

This concept of an integrated world is not a new one; it is just a more recognized one. Previous books on online work in mental health hint towards it (Fenichel, 2004), and other mental health professionals have created whole models around it, such as E-Quest (Suler, 2002), which aims as part of its remit to 'integrate online activities with in-person lifestyle' (ibid.: 379). Later chapters in this book examine the myriad of ways people now connect online for therapeutic help, as well as using static sites for information, research and self-development. For the moment, though, let us stay with the wider remit of cyberspace, as it exists at the time of writing. This Introduction aims to decipher many aspects of cyberspace, and then goes on to discuss the concept of the future of cyberspace. This theme will then be picked up as we give our concluding thoughts at the end of the book.

Websites

The wealth of information, and indeed misinformation, that exists on the Internet comes in the form of websites, collections of web pages under one domain name using hyperlinks to provide a simple route to finding whatever it is one is looking for information about. Search engines have further simplified this process in providing links to websites via Boolean terms such as OR, AND or NOT, named after George Boole, an English mathematician and philosopher. Further development of search engines came in the form of using natural language engines (see Anthony and Lawson, 2002) where search terms could be submitted using colloquial language rather than Boolean terms. Software quickly appeared which meant that individuals were able to write and upload their own websites on purchase of a domain name, on any subject from what their cat had for breakfast to an examination of the meaning of life, alongside the more notorious explosion of pornographic websites.

Email (asynchronous)

The best known aspect of Internet communication, email (electronic mail) is Simple Mail Transfer Protocol (SMTP), which is the single standard first introduced in 1982. Email is stored and forwarded by servers to network enabled devices (usually a personal computer but increasingly in mobile technology) in the time it takes to send or receive the communication. This is as opposed to device-to-device communications such as mobile SMS, which we shall cover in relation to mental health practitioners later.

Historically email could only use ASCII type characters (standard keyboard characters), but now many media formats, such as pictures, animation, video, and audio can be included in an email. Email can be sent to one or many (CC or Carbon Copied) recipients from an individual account, and often without the recipient knowing who else has received it (BCC or Blind Carbon Copied).

Listservs and forums (asynchronous)

Similar to email in many ways in as far as it is an asynchronous communication being sent via text, listservs and forums (or discussion boards or bulletin boards) utilize the public nature of the Internet to seek or disseminate information to a wider audience than just that of the intended recipient. Listservs (electronic mailing lists) deliver posted information to an inbox, and it is possible to subscribe and unsubscribe to them or alter how often the messages are posted (if at all – many choose to access such posts directly from the server itself). Forums are also web-based applications that manage user-generated content that the user has to log in to see (unless configured otherwise by the user for notifications to be delivered to an inbox). Forums contain threads (topics), which contain the posts (messages), and are usually facilitated with strict rules of conduct for members.

Chat rooms, Internet Relay Chat (IRC) and Instant Messaging (synchronous)

Chat rooms use much shorter communications held in real time so the users need to be online at the same time. Chat rooms have been usurped somewhat by Instant Messaging (IM), and both have cultural norms in Chatiquette, a sub-strand of Netiquette. Just like other forms of online communication, rules of conduct apply and public chat rooms are often monitored by the owner or volunteers, who have the power to step in and moderate users by gagging them or taking away their participation access. Chat rooms in many cases also have an audio facility, and audio files (often from popular culture) can be played to display emotion. Webcams are increasingly used in Instant Messaging, and most software can save or log the chat, even delivering messages to an inbox when the recipient is offline.

Graphical multiuser environments and virtual reality

Chat rooms that use avatars or other visuals are similar to other chat rooms except that they allow use of an avatar (a computer generated representation of, in this case, a human being) that can move around a virtual environment. These can be used for anything from simple social networking with participants simply talking to each other, to playing a multiuser game, such as World of Warcraft (WoW), where users band together to defeat enemies and achieve goals within the game. More sophisticated environments which are created by the user within a given platform, offer even more, allowing whole communities to be built, with provision of software to allow virtual sex, and some even having their own commerce, such as Second Life where the currency – which can be converted to actual currencies offline – is Linden Dollars (L$).

Blogs and blogging

Blogs (web logs) are online diaries or journals, with either full or more private public access on the Internet. The two main types of blog are personal blogs and corporate blogs. The former can be used in many different ways for the individual, such as letting people know their innermost thoughts and feelings, or as a journal to disseminate information that the individual enjoys or feels is important. Corporate blogs are more generally used to disseminate information about a company or for marketing, branding, advertising and public relations purposes. Blogs are traditionally text based, but increasingly use video, at which point they are called Vlogs. Blogs can also be defined by their purpose, such as asking questions (Qlog) or to discuss art (Artlog). All types of blog are part of the Blogosphere in cyberspace. Most blogs allow the reader to make comments on what is posted, often generating long threads of discussion and debate, particularly in the academic field.

More recently, mini-blogging has come about with websites such as Twitter, where the communication can only have a maximum of 140 characters. Tweets (the communications) are posted and witnessed by those who choose to 'follow' you. Tweets are in response to the (current) question 'What are you doing?' but in addition are often links of interest to other material on the Internet. Twitter may also be considered a social networking site, and updates can be sent to mobile devices (see Grohol, 2009).

Social and professional networking

Social networks are online communities of people who share interests, activities, friendship, family, or who are getting back in touch with people they have known in the past or friends of friends. Recently there has been a flurry of professional networking sites for people with common professional fields or interests, or for those seeking jobs via networking. Most networking sites provide a variety of ways for users to interact, such as email, IM, file sharing, mini-applications to share, such as games or contests, in-groups, fanclubs, and virtual gift giving. Professional networks can be an extremely cost-effective way of promoting start-up businesses and gaining publicity through contacts, since the majority are free to users and are funded (usually) through advertising on the site (see Lee, 2009). Notifications of the activities of other users one is linked to in relation to what one is interested in can be configured to arrive in inboxes for instant updating.

Wikis

Wikis (Hawaiian for 'fast') are simply information web pages that are held online and are open to adding to or editing by anyone who cares to do so. However, instead of being as random as it sounds, wikis encourage a collaboration of users to invest in making the information added to or edited as robust as possible for the greater good of the Internet itself. The additions and edits on wikis are also open to the same process via a simple (supplied) markup text system. Large global wikis such as Wikipedia are a good source of information if used responsibly, and smaller wikis are invaluable for many community and business websites in disseminating information in the spirit of collaboration in working towards a universal goal.

Web 2.0

What is interesting about several of the above facets of cyberspace is they demonstrate Web 2.0 in action. Netizens are involved in online communities and have a philosophy that is conducive to the development and growth of the Internet via open access and free speech. In addition, the online community has its own culture in the use and understanding of Netiquette. The online community is Web 2.0 in action.
    According to Wikipedia (2009):

> The term 'Web 2.0' describes the changing trends in the use of World Wide Web technology and web design that aim to enhance creativity, communications, secure information sharing, collaboration and functionality of the web. Web 2.0 concepts have led to the development and evolution of web-culture communities and hosted services, such as social-networking sites, video sharing sites, wikis, blogs, and folksonomies. The term first became notable after the O'Reilly Media Web 2.0 conference in 2004. Although the term suggests a new version of the World Wide Web, it does not refer to an update to any technical specifications, but rather to changes in the ways software developers and end-users utilize the Web.

The implications of Web 2.0 philosophy in the mental health field will be examined further in the final chapter. What is an unknown, however, is the evolutionary phase of the development of the Internet that is referred to as Web 3.0. This is speculative and undefinable at the moment both for practical reasons and because of lack of technological advancement. Further, constantly updating wiki discussion of Web 3.0 should be available at Wikipedia, although interestingly the information available was deleted at the time of writing.

Finally, we hope you enjoy the book as well as finding it an invaluable practitioner resource in building, developing or researching an online presence.

REFERENCES

Anthony, K. and Lawson, M. (2002) 'The Use of Innovative Avatar and Virtual Environment Technology for Counselling and Psychotherapy', in *KateAnthony.co.uk*. Available at www.kateanthony.co.uk/InnovativeAvatar.pdf [accessed 3 April 2009].

Berners-Lee, T. (1998) 'The World Wide Web: A Very Short Personal History', in *W3C World Wide Web Consortium*. Available at www.w3.org/people/berners-lee/shorthistory.html [accessed 3 April 2009].

Fenichel, M. (2004) 'Online Behavior, Communication and Experience', in R. Kraus, J. Zack and G. Stricker (eds), *Online Counseling: A Handbook for Mental Health Professionals*. San Diego: Elsevier.

Grohol, J. (2009) 'The Psychology of Twitter', in *PsychCentral*. Available at http://psychcentral.com/blog/archives/2009/02/23/the-psychology-of-twitter/ [accessed 4 April 2009].

Hauben, M. and Hauben, R. (1997) *Netizens: On the History and Impact of Usenet and the Internet*. Los Alamitos, CA: Wiley-IEEE Computer Society Press.

Lee, D. (2009) 'Making Money on a Social Network', in *BBC News*. Available at http://news.bbc.co.uk/1/hi/technology/7914351.stm [accessed 4 April 2009].

McLeod, J. (1994) 'The Research Agenda for Counselling', *Counselling*, 5(1): 41–3.

Nagel, D.M. (2008) 'Filling the Void in the Virtual Consulting Room', *Voices,* 44(3): 98–102.

Suler, J. (2002) 'E-Quest', in *The Psychology of Cyberspace*. Available at www-usr.rider.edu/~suler/psycyber/equest.html [accessed 4 April 2009].

Suler, J. (2004) 'The Online Disinhibition Effect', in *CyberPsychology and Behaviour*, 7(3): 321–6.

Wikipedia (2009) 'Web 2.0', in *Wikipedia, The Free Encyclopedia*. Available at http://en.wikipedia.org/wiki/Web_2.0 [accessed 3 April 2009].

1
THEORETICAL ASPECTS OF ONLINE THERAPY

INTRODUCTION

While it may seem elementary, we shall start with consideration of the definition of therapy itself. Many practitioners in the mental health field argue that *online* therapy is not, in the true sense of the word, psychotherapy or counseling. Penguin's *Dictionary of Psychology* offers these definitions:

> **Counselling**: a generic term that is used to cover the several processes of interviewing, testing, guiding, advising, etc. designed to help an individual solve problems, plan for the future, etc....var. *counseling*. (Reber and Reber, 2001: 162)

> **Psychotherapy**: in the most inclusive sense, the use of absolutely any technique or procedure that has palliative or curative effects upon any mental, emotional, or behavioural disorder. In this general sense, the term is neutral with regard to the theory that may underlie it, the actual procedures and techniques entailed and the form and duration of treatment ... in the technical literature the term is properly used only when the treatment is carried out by someone with recognised training and using accepted techniques ... the term is often shortened to *therapy* ...' (Reber and Reber, 2001: 586–7)

Clearly, given these definitions, one can see that therapy delivered online, regardless of 'techniques entailed' or the 'form and duration of treatment', by a therapist with recognized training, is engaged in the art and practice of counseling and psychotherapy. It is important to bear in mind that online therapy involves a different method of delivery to more traditional methods, but the therapeutic process remains the same.

With that said, this chapter will discuss online therapy from the point of view of three major theoretical orientations, which experience shows work well online, albeit in different ways. The theories we shall concentrate on are psychodynamic perspectives, humanistic perspectives, and using cognitive-behavioral methods. Before even turning on a computer to access the Internet to provide a mental health service, it is vital to understand and appreciate how one's basic theoretical orientation and beliefs – whether the practitioner provides therapy, welfare, advice-giving or just blogging thoughts for the interest of others – can be apparent as you exist in cyberspace.

There are themes common to all theoretical orientations within mental health, but an important knowledge if one wants to be an online practitioner is that existence in cyberspace requires a full commitment to knowing oneself thoroughly and being able to recognize dynamics that come into play as communication with others without a bodily presence takes place. To put this more simply, it is the ability to be oneself, without posturing or hiding behind words, that is one of the most essential factors in developing a therapeutic relationship when working online. To that end, it is this congruence with the actual self that enables a presence in cyberspace that is as fully part of an 'I–You' (Buber, 1923/1970) relationship as would occur when doing client work in the physical world.

When one sits with face-to-face clients, the successful relationship will only be possible if one can, within the boundaries of any therapeutic situation, be oneself. It is using the self to develop a mutual bond of trust and respect that will allow the client to use the relationship to explore their issues and work towards a better understanding of how those issues fit into their lives and can be coped with in order to sustain better mental health. The belief that the good therapeutic relationship between the client and the practitioner is the central element in enabling them to move on with their lives is generally considered to be an accepted position in the current therapy climate (Hick and Bien, 2008), and has a good evidence base in literature review as being the case in over 1,000 studies (Paul and Haugh, 2008).

Examining working in cyberspace from different theoretical perspectives and models is a fascinating process. It is sometimes easy to be skeptical about the modality being a fertile ground to develop a meaningful relationship with another human being or beings, when the relationship is conducted via a keyboard, mouse and screen. Critics of the online relationship as valid still exist (see reader's responses to Nagel, 2008). And yet,

> I believe I am the same person in cyberspace as I am within what is sometimes, paradoxically, called Real Life (RL). The fact that I exist within my writing over the Internet is what is important here, not the fact that I write. I use writing to convey myself to others because it is the easiest form of communication that currently exists on the Internet, just as the simplest form of communication face-to-face is the spoken word. I don't use technology for my professional work for the sake of using technology; it is just the communication system that works best for me for that client at that time. (Anthony, 2009)

So, that stated, we can move on to consider how our knowledge of therapeutic theory can be applied to working with text, from a humanistic, psychodynamic and cognitive-behavioral perspective. It is for the readers to experience each facet of the theory for themselves as they travel through cyberspace and build their experience of client work, and learn to adjust their own traditional theoretical orientation to allow for the sometimes different meaning that can be brought to the theory when working in a non-traditional setting such as working online. It is an exciting and challenging arena for theorists to explore.

HUMANISTIC PERSPECTIVES

The humanistic, or person-centered, approach to counseling is one of the orientations that sits best with this modality of communicating with a client, for precisely the reasons stated in the introduction to this chapter – its intrinsic belief that it is the client and therapist relationship that is central to the work. In considering the origins of this orientation in the work of Carl Rogers, and his belief in the work being client-led rather than practitioner-led, it is easy to see the correlations with the history of online therapy. This similarity is seen in the modality existing, developing, and growing almost entirely because there is a type of client who demands it, whether for reasons of necessity or preference over face-to-face or telephone work. Online work is usually a client-led experience rather than a referral experience – it is the client's choice if and how to work in this way.

Mearns and Thorne (1988) point out that person-centered counseling is often patronizingly thought of as an orientation that embodies everything that a good therapist should be anyway, 'before, that is, they pass on to deploy much more sophisticated techniques which can *really* deal with the client's problems' (p. 5 emphasis in the original). In examining how person-centered or humanistic theory applies to online work before looking at aspects of CBT and psychodynamic theoretical application, it should be stressed that it is the integration of each orientation, *as it applies to the professional development of the practitioner*, that forms an ethical and effective way of working when using the Internet. One of the central tenets of humanistic work – the therapist's use of the self – is also central to the online practitioner. In this way, we can see why online work is inappropriate for the novice or inexperienced therapist (Anthony and Goss, 2009) – without the journey to self-acceptance and love that is gained through training, personal therapy and experience in working with clients, it is dangerous to try to create and maintain a solid therapeutic relationship using only text. It is the belief in and love of the self that frees the therapist to convey the core conditions of Rogerian theory in a modality that seems to preclude it at first glance.

When working with text over the Internet, the therapist's use of a strong, self-knowing persona is what enables the communication to free the client into therapeutic movement towards whichever place in their lives they want to be. The therapist's trust in what they are experiencing as being valid and important, and conveying this to the client, is central to the work. Obviously, this needs careful choice of words, and usually plenty of clarification, to ensure that the client can feel the accepting and respectful understanding where traditionally it could be conveyed by a look, a gesture, or a tone of voice.

Empathy

One of the core conditions is that the practitioner is not only able to have an empathic understanding of the client, but can also communicate this to the client. When working with text, it seems obvious to state that the communication of empathy seems intensely limited – and indeed, early critics of the method indicated this, suggesting that practitioners were likely only to cut and paste the client's typing in order to reflect back to them what the client was going through and 'therapeutic interactions may be reduced to mere advice giving when face-to-face interactions are translated to the electronic medium' (Pelling and Reynard, 2000: 71). This view negates the concept of what is going on in the text-based therapeutic relationship – that the relationship exists first and foremost, and the technological base for communication is incidental, through necessity or preference. It is often useful to have the ability to use the client's words verbatim during the work, rather than attempting to paraphrase, sometimes erroneously, a previously expressed comment – but it dismisses the fact that the client is communicating with a human being rather than a computer program.

In many cases where the client has chosen to work online, there is already a sense of isolation in their lives for many different reasons. This could be the wheelchair user whose access to many physical spaces is already limited in a non-wheelchair friendly environment, the client with agoraphobia which means that leaving the house is difficult, or the client who cannot bear to communicate with another human being while being in their physical presence and having to look them in the eye. Being sensitive to clients' situations and being able to put oneself into their shoes is a skill in itself, already familiar to the reader. But being able to convey this to a client through typed text, and therefore diminishing their sense of being alone, is a skill that takes time and training to develop. This development takes the shape of not only being able to communicate using the written word effectively, but also being able to trust that the empathy felt for the client is correct without the further physical clues that occur when working face-to-face. Furthermore, the client who exists in cyberspace need not be isolated when access to the rest of the world is available to them through technological solutions, and this can often have a positive affect on their lives outside cyberspace, for example, in gaining confidence within relationships. Add to this a therapeutic relationship that contains the core conditions, including empathy, and the client is no longer alone where it counts – in their thoughts and feelings about existing in the world.

Consider this response to a client whose lack of control over her anger leads to her destroying her possessions, and whose violence has led to isolation from friends and family. This client feels vulnerable in the face of her own behavior and cannot understand why she breaks things and is seen as a person to be afraid of by those she holds close:

> It is very difficult when we do not understand why we feel this way. Often we feel frightened, alone and unable to talk about these emotions. Then what can happen is that these feelings all become too much to keep inside … it's like we need a way of releasing this pain. Sometimes our need to break things can reflect our own sense of feeling a little broken inside. (Brooks, 2003: 2)

This response from the therapist demonstrates how she has put herself in the client's position and used her empathic skills to reflect back to the client that, not only does she understand, but that the client is also not alone in her feelings. For possibly the first time, another human being has recognized that there is a person who is hurting rather than one who wants to hurt. In addition, these words of empathic understanding now actually have a physical presence in that they exist on a screen and can be printed off and kept, which the client can then re-read when her feelings overwhelm her and know that not only is there someone who understands and supports her, but that she can often stop the behavior by being able to examine her feelings rather than acting on them violently.

The client who has an empathic online therapist is no longer estranged from the human race. They are understood, have access to that understanding 24 hours a day in the printed word, and know that they are journeying with another human being with the skills and willingness to put themselves in their shoes and work together towards their better mental health. As the relationship grows and the communications flow, online therapists become more sure that their empathic understanding is true and will need less and less to check with the client that they have understood them correctly. In combination with the other core conditions of humanistic therapy, the written therapeutic relationship becomes extraordinarily powerful.

Unconditional positive regard

Conveying the potential for the therapist to have unconditional positive regard for the client is a process that can often start before any communication actually takes place when working online, through the use of the website to explain what this means and what regard the therapist *already* feels for the website visitor without having met them. This sounds facile, but it is the tone that is taken via the text while writing the website content that can convey this. Many people make the mistake of writing website content for themselves and how they would like to be, rather than being congruent (which we shall come on to) and writing for their potential client, considering the likely state of mind of the potential client. One can convey to the client that one expects to hear issues and problems that the client may feel embarrassed or ashamed of, and that as their therapist, one will think no less of them for having shared those issues. The website can state up front that the visitor is held in the utmost regard, that they are accepted and that there is a space for them to explore themselves and grow from the experience while being safe from being judged or ridiculed.

It is important to remember that the client can carry the therapist's input, literally, at all times, and therefore the text must be carefully constructed to avoid any ambiguous meaning that the client can use to fuel any self-fulfilling prophecies that she or he may have. Conveying unconditional positive regard throughout the email or IRC session can aid the interpretation of the text around it, which is often misread, unconsciously, to suit the client's agenda (Goss and Anthony, 2003). Acknowledging the client's worth and one's respect for them often renders misinterpreted text as incongruent and so the client will go back and re-read the text to better understand the meaning, as the misinterpreted text does not seem to 'fit' with their experience of the therapist thus far. In this way, the regard the practitioner holds for the client and the ability to ensure she or he understands this, underpins the whole tone of the text.

The online disinhibition effect (Suler, 2004), further defined in Chapter 2, often means that the more distressing or uncomfortable issues come up much earlier than they would in face-to-face sessions, and the practitioner may find that they are struggling with this information before they really 'know' the client and are able to feel that the unconditional positive regard is inherently in place. This process is crucial to the effectiveness of the therapeutic process – if one is not able to keep the reassurance of understanding and regard in place, the client will feel that they have 'gone too far' and they can be lost, since 'disappearance' on the Internet is facilitated so easily. It is important to indicate that, in the case of emails and forums, although a word count or length limit is appropriate, it does not mean that the content of the work is limited. Having unconditional positive regard for them means that you can trust that the pertinence of the work will emerge as the relationship grows, and that even where there is uncomfortable work going on at an early stage, this is not only expected, but welcomed.

Many humanistic or person-centered therapists will convey warmth and regard in a variety of physical ways, including smiling, appropriate touching, or leaning towards the client. Chapter 3 will focus on how this is done when working with text, but it is important to point out now that most of the physical tools that the person-centered therapist employs are entirely possible when working without a physical presence in cyberspace, even appropriate hugging (in fact, particularly hugging (Anthony, 2000)). It should be noted that representation of physical contact or movement should be encouraged when online to assist the development of the relationship and convey the core conditions of humanism. The consistency of this warmth and regard will be important as the work continues, and any withdrawal of it will rebound negatively on the work. It is therefore essential that all representation of being a physical being is natural and personal, so that it occurs without thought or specific intention, unforced. This is only possible through the vital facet of online work, as mentioned at the start of the chapter, which is congruence.

Congruence

It is not enough to ensure that the text written to the client is an accurate reflection of what the practitioner is feeling inside in response to them, which implies that congruence is something that you are forcing into the work. Trusting one's inner state and letting it flow throughout the work is essential, and as such it should go unnoticed. For example, much of the authors' own therapeutic work offline utilizes humor, and it would be incongruent not to use it online. But it is only in reflection on the text that the humor becomes apparent, it flows within the sessions without being forced. If one were to try to be witty in the session because experience shows that it can be a useful tool, there is a lack of congruence and the lack of being genuine becomes blatantly obvious to the client. This in turn affects the relationship and damages not only that but also the work that has gone before, with the client thinking that if something doesn't ring true, perhaps it has all been a sham. This is intrinsic to the concept that using the Internet and text for therapy is merely a communication tool, not a method that is used for the sake of it.

Being genuine when working in cyberspace often means experiencing a perceived sense of safety with disinhibition, for the therapist as well as the client. This is not to suggest that self-disclosure by the therapist is any more appropriate, but rather that being congruent can often mean that disclosure of personal information is often seen as a way of being genuine where it would be inhibited in a face-to-face situation. Few clients want or need to hear a therapist's history, but a reference to personal information can often help the client feel they are understood. An example of this is where the therapist, in response to the client's fears that her mothering is not good enough, allows that client to know that she is also a mother and has experience of those issues.

In the same way that forcing congruence is damaging, withholding it is equally detrimental. In a situation where laughing out loud (LOL) in a face-to-face session is appropriate, it is not inappropriate to do this within an online session – the practitioner just uses the text to convey this rather than the voice, because in cyberspace the text *is* the voice. If the therapist were not to do this, because acronyms can often feel or appear trite to the untrained or inexperienced inhabitant of cyberspace, they are not being congruent. A further example is that of hugging the client online – where personally instigating a hug at the end of a face-to-face session would not be appropriate, it would not be so online either. However, where the client would instigate this face-to-face, and reciprocating is comfortable, it is a facet of congruence that is also applicable to online work – therefore returning a hug would be appropriate (see Chapter 3).

A further consideration under this heading is that of the client's congruence. An obvious, and lazy, criticism of online work is 'how can you know that the client isn't lying?' Responses usually point out that this can't be known for sure in face-to-face sessions either, but unconditional positive regard for the client means that the practitioner trusts them and will work with whatever the client presents. However, it is important to note that when a client is using the text to deceive within an otherwise congruent relationship on both sides, it is usually easy to spot, much like a forced physical laugh to hide pain is easy to spot. Having the skill to take risks in these situations, and bearing in mind that disinhibition can often make for clumsy intervention, is where the therapist's congruence and trust in the self becomes paramount in order to get the work back on track and examine why the client has felt it necessary to hide the true situation and his or her feelings.

Psychodynamic perspectives

It is not the place of this book to discuss the intrinsic value of psychodynamic theory or indeed necessarily to describe it at length – but these theoretical concepts are useful and interesting in relation to working online and without a physical presence. Simply put, the psychodynamic approach relies on knowledge of a client's past shedding light on what is happening in the present, and with online therapy there is a wealth of rich material going on that can make for better understanding of a situation and the client's reaction to it. The unconscious processes that are occurring within the client's life and the examination of it within an online session can make for a fascinating interpretation of a client's psyche for the therapist with an interest in psychodynamic theory, which in turn can aid the therapeutic process.

Offering interpretations using the written word is a skill that takes time and care within a strong therapeutic relationship, and this should not be underestimated. The potential for offering premature interpretations that are potentially damaging for the client who will experience them outside of a face-to-face relationship, is huge, and this is particularly true in the case of the therapist's disinhibition facilitating clumsy interpretation. The speed at which online therapy tends to develop also makes for misunderstanding the level at which the client is ready to read and absorb, let alone use, an interpretation. However, done well, the use of unconscious processes and communicating this effectively to a client in writing can make for an effective shift in their thought processes. Unconscious patterns can develop in the written word as well as the spoken word, and attention can be made to consistent spelling errors ('Freudian typos') that can unlock realms of powerful imagery to aid the work. An example of this experienced by one of the authors is the client who consistently referred to the fact that her husband thought she was a 'slly' woman and that that was unbearable, a typo that put quite a different emphasis on the potential meaning of whether the hurt was caused by him thinking she was sly or silly. Not taking this typo at face value and paying attention to it developed much work, with the client assessing that 'being sly is a clever thing to be and therefore not silly at all – I prefer that'. By playing with the word via text, she was able to reframe it as something to be manipulated, and therefore less distressing.

It is possible to speculate wildly on how and where psychodynamic theory comes into play when existing in cyberspace, from the fantasies the client has about the therapist that she or he can neither hear nor see, to the transference and projection issues that the therapist has towards his or her own hardware and where this gets confused with the content of the email. By discussing some psychodynamic concepts here in relation to the online therapeutic relationship, we hope to open up some ideas around what is happening as the process develops, and so allow the work to become an enriching and fulfilling process.

Issues of transference and counter-transference

Transferential issues are an interesting concept when applied to online work, because in addition to the usual process for both the client and the practitioner, there is an added dimension to it in the form of the modality – that is, the hardware and software used to communicate. John Suler (1998, para. 10) in his paper 'Mom, Dad, Computer' argues, 'we recreate in our relationship with the computer some ASPECT of how we related to our family members' (author's use of capitals). Reactions (usually over-reactions) to email are often affected by how well hardware is performing and it takes a keen awareness of this in ensuring frustrations are not transferred to the communication. This sounds glib, but technological performance, or lack of it, can often provide interesting material within a therapeutic relationship.

If technological breakdown prevents a response getting to a client, their reaction in feeling let down, or ignored, or rejected, despite the reason for the lack of communication being entirely practical, often opens up the basis for examining where those transferential feelings are coming from. A further example is when the client's perception of availability over the Internet is as its being unlimited, as is the Internet itself, and makes for an idealization of the therapist as the perfect parent – available to the client 24 hours a day, seven days a week, for eternity. When this breaks down, it is often unbearable for the client in relation to being let down by the parent. This process is usually entirely unconscious and it is vital that the online practitioner remains aware of the potential for this happening in the simple event of technological breakdown.

Counter-transference online can also be realized by the therapist's reaction to the technological modality. In face-to-face work, the therapist can often only be contacted between certain hours on a certain day of the week – in other words, boundaries are in place. On the Internet, therapists can be contacted asynchronously around the clock and conceptually this is an exhausting prospect. Even though one can choose when to open client emails and choose when to respond, the act of being an online therapist means that at any point, and from anywhere in the world, someone may be talking to you as they compose their emails. This feeling of being always available to a client, and any possible resentment of that, may impinge on feelings towards the client when the therapist composes their responses, and this is a concept that should be borne in mind constantly.

Fantasy

We have already seen where the fantasy of the therapist as an ideal parent is apparent and useful in examining transferential issues, but the fantasy of the other person or persons in a therapeutic setting is another facet of the dynamic which should be paid attention to. Many practitioners have photos and descriptions of their personal circumstances posted on their websites, but these static images and words can never fulfill what the client wants to believe about their therapist. There is a fantasy of the therapist going on in any face-to-face relationship, of course, but without a physical presence or voice, the client often forms an idealized picture of the person who is sharing their journey – there are many gaps that the client wants to fill, and the picture they develop over the course of the relationship can vary in accuracy. With no physical clues given on a website, even the gender of the therapist can be mistaken if the name is ambiguous (Kim, Sam, Chris, etc.), and initial emails can set up a seriously erroneous fantasy that has the potential to be shattered when the truth emerges, often because the therapist has assumed the client 'knows' about him or her, and the relationship is often irreparably damaged. Consider the experience of a journalist, Sue Webster, who explored the concept of receiving online therapy and opened a therapeutic relationship with Kim Smith of www.onlinecounselling.co.uk. She had a fantasy that she was talking to a woman, writing:

If it's hard to describe what took place in those sessions, that is only because the intangibles in any therapeutic relationship are its main point. But I felt accepted and understood, no matter how shocking or shameful the situations I posed might be. Of course I didn't see or hear Kim, but I responded to her challenges and felt her empathy. If I shilly-shallied with excuses, she saw through them; if I was self-pitying, she was ironic; but if I was honest and thoughtful, she seemed to embrace me through her words. She was the wise, generous mother I had always wished for.

Although I knew on one level that this idealisation was a fantasy, I still felt let down when I eventually made telephone contact with her. In fact, I was absolutely furious. Kim Smith is a man. A very nice, sympathetic man with a northern accent who used to live on a boat and admits to wearing sandals with socks. He wasn't what I had in mind – but once I had adjusted to the new reality, I had to admit that this was surely a positive aspect to online counselling. (Webster, 2001: paras. 14–15)

Clients also have a fantasy about how their therapist sounds, reportedly sometimes giving them a voice that is calm, slow and gentle because that is how they read the emails or text chat as it appears on the screen in front of them.

All these fantasies have important implications for the therapist who feels that meeting face-to-face is viable at some point in the relationship – this can often damage the relationship because it is based on a fantasy of the practitioner that is the representation that works best for the client's therapeutic growth. We do not mean to suggest that it is ethical for a practitioner to deliberately mislead a client in allowing them to continue with a fantasy that is plainly wrong, once discovered, but the construction of a fantasy therapist, while allowing for the congruence of them to be apparent, can often help the therapeutic relationship enormously, because the reality of the physical presence (and all the biases inherent in that) is rendered redundant.

Many online practitioners will allow the client's visualization along, describing the physical environment that they are typing in (Anthony, 2000). This will feed the client's fantasy of them in a (usually) calm and controlled environment, possibly with sunshine flooding through the window and gentle music playing in the background, the aroma of fresh coffee percolating on the side of a mahogany desk as the therapist composes the response to an email. That the reality is quite different is immaterial, it is an idealized picture that is not possible in a face-to-face relationship, and therefore can be constructed by the client to aid their improvement.

Denial

The ability to work with issues of denial, and challenge, in online work is often more dynamic than in face-to-face work, simply because once the words are 'spoken', they don't fade away or get ignored – they are there in black and white on the screen or the printed page. The client's inner turmoil in repressing uncomfortable feelings and emotions is usually relieved by even the act of typing the repressed feelings, and the argument that online work is futile because the client can always rewrite themselves to appear better to the therapist is one that doesn't really hold water. If the client types something, considers it, decides it is too much to admit to and then deletes the words, they have often brought it out of their unconscious by this act even though it is too early to vocalize it to another human being (by pressing the send button). In any case, this is often not the case when online clients are composing their work because of the disinhibition effect – the perceived safety of the distance between them and the therapist makes them much more willing to admit the uncomfortable thoughts. Some chat software programs provide a function whereby you can see what the other party is typing as they type it, which means that deleted words can be seen as well. This is not recommended for therapeutic work; firstly as it could arguably be intrusive if clients do want to change their text, and secondly because it is distracting within a therapeutic session if you are watching for changes to the text.

Jacobs (1988) draws attention to the importance of the skill required to confront clients in challenging patterns of behavior, and this is no less the case in online therapy, and is possibly even more important in this context. The client who is resisting change by rejecting accurate interpretations or challenges has many options not usually available to them in a face-to-face relationship. It is easy to change an email address or username such that they cannot be traced if they decide to end the relationship after such a challenge. It is even easier to hit a disconnect button or 'hide' in a synchronous text session. The anxiety for the online therapist in this situation is usually high – if a client wishes to leave a face-to-face session, there are often physical clues to this before they actually get up and leave the room. However, in online work, there are usually just two pieces of evidence that this has happened – a notification that a client ★★★has left the chatroom★★★ or a bounced back email. Even then, the therapist has no idea whether this is a technical breakdown or not. If it is not a technical breakdown, careful examination of what was going on in the session before they left is needed and learnt from, although the empathic therapist should be in tune enough with the client to know whether the challenge was appropriate or not at that point.

Displacement and projection

Displacement and projecting feelings onto others also have their own space online, and this is usually most evident in group forum work, where each member's defense mechanisms all come into play within the group dynamic. It takes a skilled facilitator to untangle what is going on when conflict occurs in an online group, which is discussed further in Chapter 8. The client who writes 'no-one ever responds to me, even seems to understand me, let alone *like* me, so why do I bother?' can be projecting his feelings of self-worth quite effectively. In the same way, displacing feelings of anger and turning them towards the therapist is very possible, particularly in email or forum work because the therapist has no immediate avenue of response and the client has the safety of distance and time lag. Again, this is where the therapist has to be extremely careful in extracting from the text exactly what is going on and being sure that his or her own defenses do not get in the way of the work. Boundaries, which we shall discuss later in depth, are paramount here because the therapist has to take into account whether they are in a therapeutic space of their own that is as comfortable as if they were in a face-to-face environment, and comfortable enough to deal with these issues.

COGNITIVE-BEHAVIORAL THERAPY (CBT) TECHNIQUES

Cognitive-Behavioral Therapy is often seen as ideally suited to online work, because of the nature of it as being a focused and a more direct way of working – often essential when working online. The premise of CBT is that by reframing how we perceive life events we can make them less disturbing or traumatic (Beck, 1979). The concept of 'homework' in CBT ensures that the client is putting what he or she learns into practice, such as by writing assignments and self-monitoring using written ABC forms to challenge negative assumptions (A = Activating Event, B = Beliefs about that event, C = Consequences). Such work between synchronous sessions is ideally suited to online work as it can be emailed or sent before the next session and allows more room in the session to work on the written material and define new strategies within the therapy for the next set of homework required.

Michenbaum, in an interview for Derrig-Palumbo and Zeine (2005) emphasizes the importance of psycho-educational websites for clients as an adjunct to other forms of help, such as medication or more traditional delivery of therapy. In this case, psycho-education is as much about empowerment of the client in their recovery than anything else. Modeling is another important strategy for cognitive-behavioral therapists and their clients, which can be streamed from a website or supplied as a podcast. Andersson (2009) reports a CBT approach that gives the presentation of text via web pages with ongoing therapeutic support via email. Another similar example is taking place at the University of North Carolina, Chapel Hill (Hughes, 2008). A study is being conducted using internet-based CBT as an intervention for bulimia. In this study, clients are given information on web pages that would typically be given in workbook form. Instead, the clients read the workbook information online. The CBT text material is augmented with weekly group chat sessions facilitated by a therapist and hosted on a secure server. Other CBT practical strategies exist, such as the use of computers in art therapy (Malchiodi, 2000).

While not solely cognitive-behavioral approaches, homework assignments fall within the arena of focused interventions, regardless of the theoretical orientation of the actual assignment. Psycho-education and bibliotherapy are techniques that work very well with online clients, again from any theoretical orientation. The Internet is a perfect haven for a therapist to be able to utilize literature, both poetry and prose, to educate the client. Psycho-education approaches with written homework assignments lend themselves additionally to creating an evidence-based approach. Therapists whose treatment plans follow objective and measurable goals rely heavily on techniques pulled from cognitive-behavioral theory, brief solution-focused therapy, psycho-education and bibliotherapy.

Other brief approaches are adaptable to online work. For instance, Employee Assistance Programs base most of their counseling approach on cognitive-behavioral and solution-focused techniques and when delivering these services online, the same solution-focused strategies are applicable. These strategies can be implemented by therapists working in other settings as well. O'Hanlon and Beadle's (1999) 'Possibility' Therapy and Cohen-Posey's (2000) *Brief Therapy Client Handouts* are good examples of techniques and tools ideal for short-term therapy delivered online. Possibility Therapy for example, combines aspects of Roger's humanistic approach with the directive approaches of Erickson and strategic therapies with an overall solution-focused approach (O'Hanlon, 2007). Possibility Therapy interventions can be easily adapted to text-based therapy. Cohen-Posey (2000) offers a book of brief therapy handouts on a wide range of topics. The book includes a disk so that handouts can be customized. The therapist can use the handouts with online clients by adding the information as an attachment within a chat or an email.

A MODEL

It is sensible to finish with a model of online therapy based on one of the first empirical studies of online therapy that can be applied to, or considered in light of, any theoretical orientation (Anthony, 2000).

Three research questions were posed in this study of online therapy: how therapists and clients perceive the relationship as therapeutic; how the lack of visual and auditory clues are compensated for; and whether the typed word can convey the sort of therapeutic intervention that may be called therapy. The work was undertaken in view of a relationship model that considers the mutual therapeutic journey between therapist and client to be the most important facet of the process, specifically the I–You relationship, as discussed. Therefore, to conclude that the online therapy relationship may be considered therapeutic means that the relationship should contain all the facets of the I–You face-to-face relationship, as well as compensating for the fact that client and therapist are not face-to-face.

The results yielded six main themes. Four of these – rapport, presence, openness and compensation for lack of bodily presence through written communication – are presented as fulfilling the I–You therapeutic relationship. The rapport that grows through entering the client's mental constructs of the world fulfills the concept of the relationship being a mutual journey of trust, empathy and genuineness toward the client's personal growth. This is facilitated by presence, the concept that client and therapist meet in a space not limited by the computer and keyboard, having a real relationship with each other. The openness that the Internet affords contributes to the relationship being honest, and bypasses some of the defenses that the client and counselor have as well as issues of the client's shame. The quality of the written communication compensates for the lack of bodily presence via conventions of the Internet called Netiquette, and also makes for an intentional way of working with text to be therapeutic, so that from a relationship model point of view this may be called therapy.

The results also yielded two further themes. The first of these was the issue of fantasy about the therapist and client, and whether this may be considered a form of compensation for the lack of bodily presence through visual and auditory representation.

The last theme was that of the opportunity and anonymity that the Internet fosters, as a consideration of a means of having (getting to) a therapeutic relationship online.

CONCLUSION

There are, of course, many theoretical orientations – estimates range from 130 (Hackney, 2000) to over 400 (Corsini and Wedding, 2008), and it is impossible to cover all of them in relation to online work. However, most online therapists choose an eclectic approach to online work rather than a purist one, as this fits and reflects the flexibility of online work. Therefore, while a psychodynamic perspective may inform a practitioner's thoughts on a case, the work also involves an I–Thou element with all the inherent humanistic qualities contained therein, and may also include practical exercise-based work which is borrowed from CBT. Integrative approaches to online therapy fit well and, as we have already described, one can adapt a purist theoretical approach or pull from various treatment techniques, depending on the therapist, setting the best course of action for the client.

We have discussed a sampling of theoretical orientations as applied to online therapy and have concluded with the model. Now we can begin to apply this integrative approach as we examine the skills and considerations of online therapy in Chapter 2.

REFERENCES

Andersson, G. (2009) 'Using the Internet to Provide Cognitive Behaviour Therapy', in *Behaviour Research and Therapy*, 47(3): 175–80.

Anthony, K. (2000) 'The Nature of the Therapeutic Relationship Within Online Counselling', in *KateAnthony.co.uk*. Available at www.kateanthony.co.uk/thesis2000.pdf [accessed 4 April 2009].

Anthony, K. (2009) 'Cyberspace Self v. Real Self – pointless debate?' in *Online Therapy Institute Blog*. Available at www.onlinetherapyinstituteblog.com/?paged=2 [accessed 4 April 2009].

Anthony, K. and Goss, S. (2009) *Guidelines for Online Counselling and Psychotherapy, 3rd edition*. Lutterworth: BACP.

Beck, A.T. (1979) *Cognitive Therapy and the Emotional Disorders*. New York: Meridian Books.

Brooks, N. (2003) Submitted training exercise response from www.OnlineCounsellors.co.uk, used with permission.

Buber, M. (1923) *I and Thou*, tr. W. Kaufman. Edinburgh: T&T Clark, 1970.

Cohen-Posey, K. (2000) *Brief Therapy Client Handouts*. New York: John Wiley and Sons Inc.

Corsini, R.J. and Wedding, D. (2008) *Current Psychotherapies, 8th edition*. Belmont, CA: Thomson Wadsworth.

Derrig-Palumbo, K. and Zeine, F. (2005) *Online Therapy: A Therapist's Guide to Expanding Your Practice*. New York: Norton & Co.

Goss, S. and Anthony, K. (eds) (2003) *Technology in Counselling and Psychotherapy: A Practitioner's Guide*. Basingstoke: Palgrave.

Hackney, H. (2000) 'Differentiating between Counseling Theory and Process', in *ERIC Digest*. Available at www.ericdigests.org/1992-3/theory.htm [accessed 5 April 2009].

Hick, S. and Bien, T. (eds) (2008) *Mindfulness and the Therapeutic Relationship*. New York: Guildford Press.

Hughes, T. (2008) 'Internet-Based Study of Cognitive Behavioral Therapy for Bulimia to be Conducted by UNC, WPIC', in *Medical News Today*. Available at www.medicalnewstoday.com/articles/121638.php [accessed 5 April 2009].

Jacobs, M. (1988) *Psychodynamic Counselling in Action*. London: Sage.

Malchiodi, C. (2000) *Art Therapy and Computer Technology: A Virtual Studio of Possibilities*. London: Jessica Kingsley Publishers.

Mearns, D. and Thorne, B. (1988) *Person-Centered Counselling in Action*. London: Sage.

Nagel, D.M. (2008) 'Filling the Void in the Virtual Consulting Room', *Voices,* 44(3): 98–102.

O'Hanlon, B. (2007) 'Frequently asked Questions about Possibility Therapy', in *Bill O'Hanlon*. Available from www.billohanlon.com/FAQS/questionsaboutpossibilitytherapy/billohanlon.html [accessed 5 April 2009].

O'Hanlon, B. and Beadle, S. (1999) *A Guide to Possibility Land: Fifty-One Methods for Doing Brief, Respectful Therapy*. New York: W.W. Norton & Co Ltd.

Paul, S. and Haugh, S. (2008) 'The Relationship not the Therapy? What the Research Tells Us', in S. Haugh and S. Paul (eds), *The Therapeutic Relationship: Perspectives and Themes*. Ross-on-Wye: PCCS Books. pp. 9–23.

Pelling, N. and Reynard, D. (2000) 'Counseling via the Internet, Can it be Done Well?', *The Psychotherapy Review*, 2(2): 68–72.

Reber, A.S. and Reber, E.S. (2001) *Dictionary of Psychology*. London: Penguin Books.

Suler, J. (1998) 'Mom, Dad, Computer (Transference Reactions to Computers)', in *The Psychology of Cyberspace*. Available at www-usr.rider.edu/~suler/psycyber/comptransf.html. [accessed 4 April 2009].

Suler, J. (2004) 'The Online Disinhibition Effect', in *CyberPsychology and Behavior*, 7(3): 321–6.

Webster, S. (2001) 'Freudian Clicks', in *The Observer*, 18 February. Available at www.guardian.co.uk/theobserver/2001/feb/18/life1.lifemagazine8. [accessed 5 April 2009].

2
ESSENTIAL SKILLS AND CONSIDERATIONS OF ONLINE THERAPY

INTRODUCTION

When conceptualizing essential skills and considerations of online therapy, one should think in terms of the skills and considerations of both the therapist *and* the client. While many of these skills seem obvious, the dialogue in this chapter is necessary to understand fully both the therapist's responsibility to this work and the client's prerequisites for doing the work. The necessary therapist skills are above and beyond basic helping skills the therapist may have acquired through schooling, practicums, internships and employment.

DETERMINING IF ONLINE THERAPY IS RIGHT FOR THE THERAPIST

Clearly, the online therapist should have an arsenal of skills that reflect therapeutic intervention knowledge as well as hands-on, practical computer knowledge. It is not necessary for the online therapist to be an expert in technology, but it is vital that the online therapist is comfortable with certain skills and possible scenarios before taking on clients independent of supervision or consultation. If a therapist spends some time online looking for resources to enhance client progress or to learn how to improve one's private practice, learn new skills or seek professional development and networking opportunities, it is likely this person will naturally and easily adapt to online work. If, on the other hand, a therapist does not have a natural desire to use the computer and has little experience with basic transactions and interactions online, this therapist should spend time involved in the Internet culture before deciding to train in order to add online therapy to the suite of services offered.

Other ways a therapist may assess his or her match for online therapy is to think in terms of 'transferable skills'. In what other settings has the therapist worked that might imply a transfer of skills from a previous work environment to working online? Practitioners who have worked on a telephone hotline have counselled in a setting devoid of visual cues and are accustomed to the rapid rapport building that can occur via distance. Practitioners who have offered 'advice' through newspaper or magazine columns may easily adapt these skills to therapeutic email exchanges with training. For therapists who use bibliotherapy or therapeutic writing (Bolton et al., 2004) to engage clients, the Internet can be a natural next step in finding a place for cyberspace within one's practice. These are but a few examples (Nagel, 2007) that can help a therapist determine if online work is a good fit for them. Determining what methods of Internet delivery a therapist may feel best suited for is important for the therapist to consider as well. Some therapists may feel comfortable with email, others with chat. Still other therapists may determine they are only comfortable using email and/or chat as adjunct support with existing face-to-face clients.

Fenichel (2000) refers to a set of practical and emotional skills necessary for the therapist to possess, including:

- Quick or touch typing skills
- Comfort with Internet tools such as downloading programs or using various platforms and software
- Basic computer skills such as adjusting settings, configurations or adding hardware
- Toleration of the need for swift responses to clients or delays in responses from clients; ability to accumulate, store and easily retrieve web links
- Ability to receive, store and protect communication from clients
- Utilization of encryption
- Expressive writing skills
- Therapist training and a theoretical background to draw upon.

Fenichel's emotional skills list includes the following:

- Comfort in describing one's own and other's feelings with text
- Comfort with a text-only environment
- Awareness of how the client may perceive the therapist online
- Skill at clarifying online communication when necessary
- Desire to be online
- Experience with online relationships through synchronous and asynchronous methods
- Belief that relationships online via text can be meaningful and therapeutic
- Confidence with technology and tolerance for computer glitches
- Ability to use various methods of delivery (face-to-face, chat, email, etc.) depending on the needs of the client
- Ability to handle a wide range of client emotions as expressed in client text.

While this list is extensive, it is certainly not exhaustive. Nevertheless, these practical and emotional skills are needed to provide a best standard of care to the client. Therapists reviewing this list should have an immediate sense about how well suited they may be to do the work of a text-based therapist.

ADAPTING THERAPIST SKILLS TO ONLINE WORK

Most trained face-to-face therapists utilize a subset of skills related to empathic listening. A brief review of skills associated with empathic listening (Pickering, 1986) is offered here with an in-depth discussion about how these essential skills occur within text-based therapy. A further look at the embodiment of text-based therapy is given in Chapter 3 and through the case study in Chapter 6.

Attending and acknowledging provides verbal and non-verbal awareness of the other. Online, this is achieved by using text to confirm that the therapist is 'listening' by acknowledging received text. With asynchronous email, the therapist might give an immediate response upon receipt, acknowledging receipt. For instance, 'Jane, I did receive your email today and just wanted to let you know that I will respond by tomorrow. Take care …' In this way, the client has been acknowledged and attended to as soon as the therapist opened the email. Within the therapist's response email, the therapist can use additional language that indicates active and empathic listening. Within a synchronous chat, a therapist might type text to the client as an indication that the therapist 'hears' the client. One way to avoid non-therapeutic silence is to suggest to the client, 'Sometimes you may have a response or a thought which results in lengthy text. If you are comfortable, enter text as you complete a sentence or phrase and I will do the same.' Another option is to teach the client to use the phrase 'PFT, k?' ('pause for thought, okay?') when he or she needs time to respond. If the chat program offers cues that the other person is typing a response, alert the client that when either is typing, there will be an indicator. In between sentences and phrases or during a long pause in which the therapist is waiting for a response, the therapist can type words like, 'okay', 'I am still here' or 'take your time'.

Restating and paraphrasing provides responses to a person's basic messages. Reflecting back feelings, experiences or content that has been heard or perceived by the therapist may also occur in the process of paraphrasing. Offering a tentative interpretation about the client's feelings, desires or meanings can also take place. In the case of online therapy, the message is not verbal but text-based using written language. The following example combines restatement, reflection and interpretation.

The client states in an email or chat, 'Yesterday was such a hard day. I had to get the kids up, make breakfast and fight with them to get dressed on time so that I could take them to school. Then I had to dash to work and prepare for a 10:00 meeting. The meeting bled into lunch so I did not get a chance to eat and I forgot to put a protein bar in my purse. Mid-afternoon I had yet another meeting that went late and I was late picking the kids up from the after-school program. By the time I got home I was so exhausted, and I had to make dinner, then help the children with their homework, prompt them to bathe and get them in bed. I finally got a chance to do my prep work for today at 11:00 last night. I just can't go on like this.' The therapist might in turn reply, 'You had quite a busy and hectic day! It sounds like you are always trying to catch up with yourself. I can imagine being a single mother with two children and a full time job could leave you exhausted and depleted.'

Summarizing and synthesizing brings together feelings and experiences, providing focus for the client. In asynchronous emails the summary may fall at the end of the email after the therapist has offered paraphrasing, reflection and interpretation. The therapist may begin the summary paragraph with, 'As you have described your very busy day I could feel how exhausted and overwhelmed you must be. I posed some questions and offered suggestions about how you might manage your day in a way that will allow you to feel differently.' In synchronous chat, the therapist may summarize at key points within the session and certainly as the session draws to a close. For instance, after the client describes her day, the therapist might chat back, 'That sounds like a very hectic day and I can see how you might be feeling overwhelmed. I suggest we discuss for a moment how you are managing your time. Maybe together we can come up with some strategies that will help.'

Probing is questioning the client in a supportive way that requests more information or that attempts to clear up confusions. With email, when the therapist needs clarification, questions like 'Can you clarify for me what you meant when you said …?' can be used. Since chat is synchronous, the therapist can ask immediately during the session for clarification. Phrases like, 'I want to make sure I understand correctly …' and 'Are you saying …?' can prove helpful when attempting to gain clarity from a client. If the goal of probing is to gain more information, the therapist might simply ask, 'Can you tell me more about …' or 'Has this ever happened before?' The particular questions asked when seeking more information will be different depending on the case. Asking questions is a critical part of building the therapeutic alliance and gaining information to further assist the client. Questions may be asked to discover more about a client's history, to encourage the client to think in various ways about an issue, or, as in the examples above, to clarify meaning within the therapeutic conversation. In turn, the therapist encourages the client to ask questions within email or chat text.

Giving feedback is defined by Pickering (1986) as a way of sharing perceptions of the other's ideas or feelings or disclosing relevant personal information. An email that the therapist offers in response to the client's email may offer insight-oriented statements or questions to the client. The same applies to chat. Because chat is synchronous, feedback questions and statements can take place in real-time during the course of the therapy session. 'What do you think your boss would say if you told her your concern about the project she has assigned to you?' or 'I wonder if your boss would be accepting of your concern if you told her' are examples of feedback that offers insight and allows the client to engage in critical thinking about a particular issue. An example of disclosing relevant personal information includes disclosing to a mother of an adolescent girl, 'I have a 16-year-old girl as well.' This can occur within a chat session or in the body of an email to a client, for example, 'Being a mother to an adolescent girl too, I understand.'

Supporting shows warmth and caring in a therapist's own individual way. Acknowledging with words via text is first and foremost conveyed within the tone of the text. Physicality can be expressed with emotional bracketing. For instance, a therapist might utilize emotional bracketing, '[take my hand] as we talk about this' or '[smiling]' to express physical aspects of communicating emotion and adding the nuances of body language into the text dialogue. A therapist can offer a hug (Anthony, 2000) conveyed as

((((Jane)))) or the client and therapist may choose to use acronyms, emoticons, and proper attention to closures or sign-offs.

Checking perceptions involves finding out if interpretations and perceptions are valid and accurate. This can be accomplished in email and chat with phrases like, 'Correct me if I am wrong …', 'I am guessing that perhaps …' and 'Does this seem to fit?' Appropriate phrases like, 'What I hear you saying is …' or 'I understand you to mean …' can be integrated into asynchronous and synchronous communication. In a similar fashion the therapist may ask the client, 'Can you repeat back to me your understanding of what I have suggested?' or 'Can you tell me how you heard my last statement?' In this way, the therapist has a better sense as to whether or not the client has understood the therapist's intent. These are all examples of checking perceptions that, similarly, may be used in reflection and paraphrasing.

Finally, the last skill Pickering (1986) refers to is that of *being quiet* so as to give the client time to think as well as to talk. While this skill does not appear to apply as readily to therapeutic email exchanges, it should be noted that email works very well for people who wish to write, review and edit thoughts, as silence is naturally embedded into email therapy. Silence is a natural component of therapy and synchronous chat therapy is no different in this regard. When the therapist, for instance, asks a question or suggests an idea or interpretation, the client may take a moment or two to respond. In a chat setting these client words may come in one long entry taking time between posts or the words may come in short pieces, a little at a time. The therapist must 'listen' and gauge whether or not to wait for the complete thought, whether the thought arrives as one entry or in 'chunks' from the client. The therapist waits until the client has given a complete and finished thought. Then the therapist responds in the appropriate reflective manner. The therapist may advise the client to choose between typing the entire thought before submitting or entering short 'chunks' or phrases from the entire thought a little at a time. The therapist may also advise the client to type an acronym of some type such as 'pft,k' as discussed previously.

So, as we have established, active, empathic listening is a skill that is transferable to online therapy. While the therapist does not audibly listen, the therapist attends to the client in a similar way. The online therapist reads client text with focus. With email, the asynchronous communication allows the therapist to choose a time that will be void of distraction. The therapist can concentrate on the contents of the text. With chat, the therapist reads the client's chat posts as if in a conversation, but with attention to the different rhythm that occurs in chat. For instance, in face-to-face therapy it is uncommon for verbal statements from either party to occur out of order. The face-to-face conversation follows sequence, and while there may be the occasional talk that is spoken simultaneously, the flow of the conversation is forward moving. Within a therapeutic chat conversation, the therapist must pay attention to what the client is saying, and having responded, return to the client's chat entries to review any additional chat posts entered by the client while the therapist was posting a reply. This cadence in online chat is part of the uniqueness of synchronous Internet relay chat. The movement is forward and back then forward again. The therapist 'listens' and uses other essential skills to ensure the client's text is interpreted correctly, and vice versa.

Attending to body language is also possible via text-based therapy. During face-to-face therapy, a therapist pays attention to body language to gain clues about mood and affect beyond the client's self-report. Attending to body language in email and chat means listening to tone; to read and hear the text 'aloud'. By doing this one can usually sense mood and envision body posture. Other ways to pick up on body language is to watch for cues in the typed text. Is the client typing slower than usual if in chat? Is the client using all CAPS or changing usual patterns? An example might be a person who always capitalizes the pronoun 'I' and begins to use 'i' instead. The most obvious way to know the client's body language is to ask. Responses like, 'I am just so tired …' or 'This chair is hurting my back …' are indications of body language. Finally, a concrete way to describe body language within text is to use what is referred to as emotional bracketing. With emotional bracketing a client may type, 'It sure has been a long week! [sigh]' or, 'That phone call really upset me [slumping in chair].'

Teaching the client about use of language online with tools such as emotional bracketing and descriptive immediacy can add richness to the content. Emotional bracketing adds another dimension to the text in that both the client and the therapist can compensate for the lack of non-verbal communication by bracketing the emotional content behind the typed text. Important emotional content (particularly emotional information that we couldn't otherwise glean from the text) can be placed in square or other brackets (Collie, 2000).

Descriptive immediacy is a technique that is used to deepen the connection between client and therapist. The client can be encouraged to use descriptive immediacy to impart important information to the therapist. Descriptive immediacy can be used to highlight a moment of intense emotion, i.e., any situation in which a simple verbal response is not enough. This may be about a success or perhaps in response to a very painful disclosure. Descriptive immediacy can also be used in situations in which the client's words seem incongruent or contradict a previous text exchange. For example, 'As I read your last statement, I can sense how overwhelmed you must be…'. A statement like this works well to confirm the impact of an intense emotional disclosure or even mildly confront client disclosures that the client may be playing off as insignificant.

CLIENT COMMUNICATION BETWEEN SESSIONS

So far discussion has focused on using technology to communicate with clients for therapeutic purposes. Sometimes the need arises between sessions to continue the therapeutic dialogue or to assist in keeping the client on task with the goals of the therapy. Other times, between session contacts may have more to do with 'housekeeping' (scheduling or cancelling an appointment, acknowledging technology glitches) than therapy itself. Typically the therapist utilizes phone or email for housekeeping issues. However, the therapist must remain cognizant of the possibility that confidential information can be leaked even in innocuous email exchanges. Unless an encrypted email service is used, confidentiality may be compromised even when communicating about housekeeping issues or providing website links, handouts or homework exercises.

See the following email as an example:

To: couns@email.com

From: Client@email.com

Hi,

I am wondering if I can change my appointment to next Tuesday, same time. Thursday is just not going to work for me this week. Is that ok?

By the way, I really had a rough weekend. My husband and I fought all day Saturday and Sunday. I just laid around the house. Can't wait to see you so we can talk about this.

Thanks,

Jane Client

If the therapist replies to this email sent through non-encrypted channels, the client's personal information may be compromised. While it is best to use encrypted channels even for basic emails like this, if a client emails from an unencrypted email, one can remove the body of the client's email before responding or simply begin a new email with a subject line such as 'Follow Up' or 'Your Inquiry'. In the body of the email, 'Tuesday at 4:00 works fine' can simply be stated.

Identifying tag lines in the email that directly or indirectly indicate therapy services (e.g. website address, credentials after a name, etc.) may compromise confidentiality by alerting an interceptor that this correspondence is between a therapist and possible client, revealing the nature of the relationship. Therefore, using encrypted channels for all communication is essential between sessions.

Dealing with emergencies between sessions is an issue that will be more thoroughly discussed later but for the purposes of this discussion, between-session emergencies should be handled with health, safety and welfare as the most important considerations. The initial informed consent and intake process should thoroughly explain emergency procedures to the client.

For the therapist who desires to offer support between sessions, to check in, modulate intensity of emotions or offer grounding and containment to a client, a discussion about parameters and boundaries regarding online communication is paramount. The therapist should be very specific about how and why between-session contact will take place. This includes all points on the continuum between basic housekeeping and emergency contact. Keeping necessary boundaries around communication will ensure the therapeutic relationship remains professional. New online therapists may find themselves falling into a routine that is akin to a pen–pal relationship with no formal guidelines about email exchanges. Therapists who use chat may find that clients will begin a conversation at times apart from scheduled appointments. The therapist must determine individualistic ways to maintain therapeutic boundaries yet offer support in a way that fits the style and theoretical background of the therapist.

Provided the communication channels are encrypted, the following suggestions are made to offer support and encouragement between scheduled chat sessions or therapeutic email exchanges.

One obvious benefit of online work is the sharing of resources. During a face-to-face session, a therapist might say, 'This discussion reminds me of an article that you might benefit from reading. I will bring the article next week.' Online, the therapist can immediately offer the resource, or if the client is face-to-face, the therapist can opt to email the resource between sessions while the topic is still pertinent and fresh. During an online chat, if the therapist does not have the resource readily available, a between session email is an option.

Writing a journal is another option a therapist may offer the client. Journal writing as part of the therapeutic process has long been used in psychoanalysis and has been used by many therapists as an ancillary technique in therapy (Brand, 1979). It is common for people to write a journal with an intended audience in mind. Even if another will never read the journal, some people envision writing to a particular person or audience. Sometimes having an intended audience is helpful for the journaling process. If the client finds writing a journal beneficial with the therapist as the intended audience, the therapist can offer this between sessions as an option. For prolific journal writers, the therapist will not be able to read all of the material between the sessions and this can be explained to the client. 'Jane, if writing a journal would be helpful for you, feel free to journal and if you want to journal to me that is fine too. You can email me between sessions as often as you like. I cannot guarantee that I will be able to read your entries before our next session but I would like to offer this to you.' The therapist can then 'check in' during the next session or email exchange with words like, 'I received several entries from you this week. I have not read them but wanted to ask if there is an entry in particular that you would like to discuss?'

The therapist may assign 'homework' such as a worksheet or reading assignment. The homework or reading assignment may be determined to have greater impact if delivered mid-week between sessions. Or, as previously mentioned, the therapist may not have the assignment to hand and has decided to assign the material based on information that was discussed in an email exchange or a chat session. In this case, the therapist can search for applicable homework and email the client after the session or between formal email exchanges. Depending on the client and the relevance, the therapist may opt to send all or part of a chat transcript to the client to review before the next chat or face-to-face session. The use of transcripts is not a new phenomenon and has been used in therapy long before Internet Relay Chat was available (Brandell, 1990).

These homework strategies may not be part of the therapist's orientation or style but text-based information and assignments between sessions often help people stay engaged in the process. People who seek out text-based therapy generally have an affinity with the written word and appear to be more receptive to such between session strategies.

Therapists may also choose to provide brief 'check-in' emails between sessions with short sentences or affirmations where appropriate. Email removes the hierarchy in communication and clients often find this endearing and feel that the therapist is truly empathic with these between session notes. However, the therapist should formulate the boundary in advance and articulate expectations early on to avoid a client responding unnecessarily between sessions. This email process is akin to the recent use of mobile phones to send reminders or positive statements to people in recovery or who need assistance with disease management for conditions such as asthma (Neville et al., 2002) or chlamydia (Menon-Johansson et al., 2006). However, with certain text messaging technologies, the client cannot text back. Email allows the client to instantly respond by hitting reply unless the therapist has an email program that includes do-not-reply email capability.

NECESSARY CLIENT SKILLS

Certainly, just as therapists require a certain skill set to deliver therapy online, clients must also possess basic skills so that the therapy is effective and beneficial. Practical factors include accessibility, typing ability and comfort with technology (Chechele and Stofle, 2003). Therapists should also assess the client's comfort with reading and writing. Clearly, individuals considering online therapy must possess written language skills and be able to express emotion through text. It is further suggested that therapists assess whether clients have cognitive or physical issues (including mental health conditions) that might have an impact on a person's ability to read and write (ISMHO Clinical Case Study Group, 2003).

Consider the following questions from the same ISMHO resource to determine if your client has the necessary practical skills to engage effectively in online therapy:

- How might the person's computer skills, knowledge, platform and Internet access affect the therapy?
- How knowledgeable is the person about online communication and relationships?
- How well suited is the person for the reading and writing involved in text communication?
- How might physical and medical factors affect the online therapy?

Therapists can also take steps in advance of contact to allow a potential client to 'self-screen' for online therapy services. For example, a therapist's website might include statements such as 'Are you comfortable enough with technology to consider therapy in a new way?' or 'Do you like reading books, emailing and chatting online?' These statements reflect the cognitive skills necessary to engage in online therapy.

DETERMINING AT THE ONSET WHETHER ONLINE THERAPY IS SUITABLE FOR THE CLIENT

The client's practical set of skills is considered just part of the overall initial intake and assessment necessary to determine a client's suitability for text-based therapy with a particular therapist.

The questions and statements referred to above can be incorporated into a formal intake and assessment process, but, as previously stated, the therapist's website can offer information to the client as well. In this way, the assessment process is mutual and begins the instant the person seeks services from a particular therapist or e-clinic online. Along with suitable questions the therapist might pose on a website, additional information can be included as well. For instance, offering a separate web page that describes the benefits of online therapy or posting an article that offers insight about whether or not online therapy will be a good fit for the client can prove extremely helpful (Nagel, 2008a).

Other factors that must be considered when determining appropriateness for the client include an understanding of why clients may seek online therapy. Factors may include the following:

- Availability of services within a geographic area
- Perceived need for anonymity
- Need or desire for specialized services
- Lack of transportation
- Disability
- Time management
- Convenience
- Cost.

Clients who live in rural communities might not have access to appropriate clinical services and the travel distance may be prohibitive. The perceived need for anonymity might also be a factor in rural areas even if a therapist offers services locally. A person may not want to receive services from the only practitioner in a small town due to fear of others in the community finding out.

While clients should never be anonymous within contracted online therapeutic relationships, the lack of physicality may offer a sense of anonymity. The disinhibiting quality of therapy via chat or email may be appealing to certain clients. As first mentioned in Chapter 1, Suler (2004) defines a concept known as the online disinhibition effect that describes the way a person behaves on the Internet with less restraint than in face-to-face situations. Anthony (2009) summarizes Suler's definition of the disinhibition effect in this way (using Suler's headings):

You Don't Know Me (dissociative anonymity)

The Internet offers apparent anonymity – if you wish, you can keep your identity hidden and use any name, either close to your own (e.g KatAnt) or very far away (e.g Xyz123). For the most part, people only know what you choose to tell them about yourself. When people have the opportunity to separate their actions from their real world and identity, they feel less vulnerable about opening up. They also feel less need to be accountable for their actions – in fact; people might even convince themselves that those behaviors 'aren't me at all.' In psychology this is called 'dissociation'.

You Can't See Me (invisibility)

In many online environments other people cannot see you. As you browse through web sites, message boards, and even some chat rooms, people may not even know you are there at all. In text communication such as e-mail, chat, blogs, and instant messaging, others may know a great deal about who you are. However, they still can't see or hear you – and you can't see or hear them. Even with everyone's identity visible, the opportunity to be physically invisible amplifies the disinhibition effect. Invisibility gives people the courage to go places and do things that they otherwise wouldn't, often with undesirable results, but also with therapeutically valuable opportunities in therapy.

See You Later (asynchronicity)

In e-mail and message boards, communication is asynchronous. People don't interact with each other in real time. Others may take minutes, hours, days, or even months to reply to something you say. Not having to deal with someone's immediate reaction can be disinhibiting. In e-mail and message boards, where there are delays in feedback, people's train of thought may progress more steadily and quickly towards *deeper expressions* of what they are thinking and feeling in comparison to instantaneous communications. Some people may even experience asynchronous communication as 'running away' after posting a message that is personal, emotional, or hostile. It feels safe putting it 'out there' where it can be left behind.

It's All In My Head (solipsistic introjection or egoistic self-absorption)

The absence of the visual and aural cues of face-to-face communication combined with text communication can have other interesting effects on people. Reading another person's message might be experienced as a voice within one's head, as if that person magically has been inserted or 'introjected' into one's psyche, similar to how we hear a character when reading a book. In fact, consciously or unconsciously, we may even assign a visual image to what we think that person looks like and how that person behaves. The online companion now becomes a character within personal mental experience of the world. Online text communication can become the psychological tapestry in which a person's mind weaves fantasy role-plays, usually unconsciously and with considerable disinhibition.

It's Just A Game (dissociative imagination)

If we combine the feeling that all these conversations are going on inside our own heads with the nature of cyberspace as a means to escape real life, we get a slightly different force that magnifies disinhibition. People may feel that the imaginary characters they 'created' exist in a way that is quite separate from everyday life – a different realm altogether. It is possible to split or 'dissociate' online fiction from offline fact. Once they turn off the computer and return to their daily routine, they believe they can leave that game and their game-identity behind. Why should they be held responsible for what happens in that make-believe play world that has nothing to do with reality?

We're Equals (minimizing authority)

While online others may not know a person's status in the face-to-face world and it may not have as much impact as it does in that world. In most cases, everyone on the Internet has an equal opportunity to voice him or herself. Although one's status in the outside world ultimately may have some impact on one's powers in cyberspace, what mostly determines your influence on others is your skill in communicating.

People are reluctant to say what they really think as they stand before an authority figure, but online, in what feels like a peer relationship – with the appearances of 'authority' minimized – it is much easier to speak out and think, 'Well, what can they do to me?' As the Internet grows, with a seemingly endless potential for creating new environments, many people see themselves as independent-minded explorers. This atmosphere and philosophy contribute to the minimizing of authority.

If one considers the disinhibition effect, many additional personality factors may cause a person to seek online therapy services. Issues related to power, control, authority, dissociation, manipulation and delusion all may come into play.

A person might also seek specialized services online. If there is not a practitioner in the community who has expertise or specialism in a certain area, the client has the opportunity to find such an expert online. For instance, there may not be a therapist in a local geographic area that specializes in post partum depression but help may be available through online therapy with a therapist who specializes in this area.

Lack of transportation can be an issue for some people who might ordinarily seek therapy locally. In addition, disability can hinder a person's ability to engage in face-to-face therapy. The disability could be physical, creating mobility issues. People who are deaf may prefer text-based therapy if limited services are available locally. Mental disability might impair a person's ability to seek services outside the home. For instance, anxious, depressed or agoraphobic individuals may have difficulty leaving the home.

Time management and convenience are yet another reason people seek services online. With busy schedules, many people prefer the ease and convenience of online therapy. Flexibility for online appointments and the ability to pace oneself with email exchanges is appealing to a segment of the population.

Finally, individuals may seek online therapy because the cost of services is sometimes less than face-to-face therapy. While this is not always the case, some practitioners opt to lower online fees because their online practice overhead is less or to help offset the lack of insurance or subsidized coverage for the service.

Whether a practitioner is in private practice or has joined a team or e-clinic, a formal intake process should be established. Many practitioners require an 'intake form' or questionnaire at the beginning of face-to-face services and working online is no different. Issues regarding encryption and security will be addressed in Chapter 4; for the purposes of this discussion, questionnaires should be submitted via secure methods. The intake process can reflect the therapist's style and primary theoretical orientation. For instance, a psychodynamic therapist is likely to ask many questions about childhood experience while a cognitive behavioral therapist might ask about interventions or methods that have worked in the past. Integrative therapists may ask a combination of questions. With reference to the previous discussion about the reason why a client may seek therapy services online, a question reflecting the reason is warranted during the formal intake process. This question alone could provide insight about the client's comfort with the online culture, physical health and personality factors. The Intake Questionnaire can also be a formal way to gather information about the client's experience with technology. From direct questions about technology (type of platform, experience online) to the use of language when answering open-ended questions, the therapist can gain information about the client's suitability for online work.

Are you interested in traditional face-to-face therapy, online therapy or a combination of both?

☐ Face-to-face

☐ Distance

☐ Face-to-face/Distance

If you are requesting online therapy, why are you interested in online therapy rather than traditional face-to-face therapy at this point?

Please tick all that you have experience with:

☐ Email   ☐ Instant Messaging/Chat

☐ Encrypted email or chat   ☐ Blogs

☐ Chat rooms with multiple people   ☐ Bulletin Boards/Forums

☐ Payment for items/services online

☐ Social Networks

What type of platform does your computer use?

☐ Windows Vista   ☐ Windows XP   ☐ Windows   ☐ Mac OS

☐ Linux   ☐ Other: _____

What type of internet access do you have?

☐ Dial-up   ☐ Broadband (cable, DSL, satellite)

FIGURE 2.1   SAMPLE QUESTIONS THAT OFFER INSIGHT INTO A POTENTIAL CLIENT'S KNOW-HOW ONLINE AND APPROPRIATENESS FOR TEXT-BASED THERAPY (NAGEL, 2008b)

Figure 2.1 illustrates sample questions that offer insight into a potential client's know-how online and appropriateness for text-based therapy (Nagel, 2008b). See Chapter 6 for a working example of an Intake Questionnaire.

Other ways to incorporate a screening process include offering an initial consultation by voice or chat. Spending 15–30 minutes with the potential client, explaining how online work is done and asking for a general statement about what brings the client to therapy, is another good way to gain a sense of client–therapist fit. Some practitioners opt to offer consults upon request, but otherwise rely on the Intake Questionnaire. Yet other practitioners include a statement in an Informed Consent contract specifying that the first few sessions will be utilized to determine the need and fit for ongoing therapy. While there are many ways to screen a potential client for suitability, the key is actually implementing a method that is responsible to the client and ethical to the profession.

Now that we have discussed characteristics and skills of the therapist and the client and reviewed initial intake and assessment, we can discuss further the 'nuts and bolts' of the work. Chapter 3 takes a closer look at text-based therapy – the structure, the nuances, the language – working without a physical presence.

REFERENCES

Anthony, K. (2000) 'Counselling in Cyberspace', in *Counselling*, 11(10): 625–7. Available at www.kateanthony.co.uk/index.php?MenuOption=Counselling [accessed 5 April 2009].

Anthony, K. (2009) 'The Online Disinhibition Effect', in *Online Therapy Institute Blog*. Available at www.onlinetherapyinstituteblog.com/?p=298 [accessed 6 April 2009].

Bolton, G., Howlett, S., Lago, C. and Wright, J. (eds) (2004) *Writing Cures*. Hove, UK: Brunner-Routledge.

Brand, A.G. (1979) 'The Uses of Writing in Psychotherapy', *Journal of Humanistic Psychology*, 19(4): 53–72.

Brandell, J. (1990) 'Monitoring Change in Psychotherapy through the Use of Brief Transcripts', in P. Kelley (ed.), *The Uses of Writing in Psychotherapy*. New York: The Haworth Press.

Chechele, P. and Stofle, G. (2003) 'Individual Therapy Online via Email and Internet Relay Chat', in S. Goss and K. Anthony (eds), *Technology in Counselling and Psychotherapy: A Practitioner's Guide*. Basingstoke: Palgrave Macmillan.

Collie, K. (2000) 'E-Mail Counseling: Skills for Maximum Impact', in *ERIC/CASS Digest*. Available at www.ericdigests.org/2002-3/e-mail.htm [accessed 6 April 2009].

Fenichel, M. (2000) 'Online Psychotherapy: Technical Difficulties, Formulations and Processes', in Fenichel.com. Available at www.fenichel.com/technical.shtml [accessed 6 April 2009].

ISMHO Clinical Case Study Group (2003) 'Assessing a Person's Suitability for Online Therapy', in *ISMHO*. Available at www.ismho.org/therapy_suitability_assessment.asp [accessed 6 April 2009].

Menon-Johansson, A.S., McNaught, F., Mandalia, S. and Sullivan, A.K. (2006) 'Texting Decreases the Time to Treatment for Genital Chlamydia Trachomatis Infection', in *Sexually Transmitted Infection*, 82(1): 49–51.

Nagel, D.M. (2007) 'Who Can Perform Distance Counseling?', in J. Malone, R. Miller and G. Walz (eds), *Distance Counseling: Expanding the Counselor's Reach and Impact*. Ann Arbour, MI: Counselling Outfitters.

Nagel, D. (2008a) 'Is Online Counseling Right for You?', in *Ezine@rticles*. Available at http://ezinearticles.com/?Is-Online-Counseling-Right-For-You?&id=1732152 [accessed 6 April 2009].

Nagel, D.M. (2008b) 'Intake Form', in *DeeAnna Merz Nagel*. Available at www.secure-quotes.com/deeannamerznagel/intake2_form.asp [accessed 6 April 2009].

Neville, R., Greene, A., McLeod, J., Tracey, A. and Surie, J. (2002) 'Mobile Phone Text Messaging can Help Young People Manage Asthma', in *BMJ*, 325(7364): 600.

Pickering, M. (1986) 'Communication', in *EXPLORATIONS, a Journal of Research of the University of Maine*, 3(1): 16–19.

Suler, J. (2004) 'The Online Disinhibition Effect', *CyberPsychology and Behavior*, 7(3): 321–6.

3
WORKING WITHOUT A PHYSICAL PRESENCE

INTRODUCTION

In the previous chapter the essential skills and characteristics of the online therapist and the online client were examined. In addition, careful consideration was given to initial intake and assessment. Having discussed the generalities, we can now take a more detailed look at the process of text-based therapy. We will see how it is possible to convey everything that is requisite in a therapeutic relationship by only using text. The ability to do this requires not just knowledge of how people communicate in cyberspace but also the self-confidence and trust in the internal supervisor to develop and maintain an individual style and method that is congruent. In learning about the three main facets of Internet communication – Netiquette, use of emoticons, and use of acronyms and abbreviations – it is important to understand that just because they exist, it does not mean that each message has to be filled with them. In finding your personal style of communication, within the boundaries of Internet communication as a whole, you will also discover a level of communication with each client that is comfortable, meaningful and fulfilling.

APPROPRIATE EMAIL COMMUNICATION

When we sit opposite a client, our posture, facial expression, gestures and tone of voice all convey messages that either complement the words we are speaking, or actually convey a message itself. In taking away all those facets of face-to-face communication in using text to talk to someone, we are left with the stark black-on-white of the typed word. Not only that, but the ease and convenience of Internet communication makes us lazy with text, dropping capital letters and not worrying about misspellings. Email breaks down hierarchical barriers allowing for a more relaxed relationship, or one that is at least perceived as such. No longer does one have to knock on the boss's door for a moment alone; an employee can simply dash off an email and say whatever is on his or her mind. A recent popular magazine offered a deconstructive look at email communication pointing out particular concerns, from one's email address (self-promoting domain name or underscored and personal) to the difficulty in conveying sarcasm through email exchange (Krause, 2008). Suler (2004) offers a detailed analysis of message peripherals including the username, the subject line, the greeting and the sign-off, suggesting a complex anatomy of an email that includes overt communication as well as seemingly insignificant aspects of the communication that are full of covert meaning. Interpreting movement from a pseudonym to one's real name as an expressed desire to drop the mask of anonymity and the repeated use of 're:' in the subject line as a reflection of the passive indifference the writer has to the relationship, are two examples Suler offers. He further suggests that the lack of a formal greeting implies the sender has no particular interest in pursuing a personal connection while 'Dear Jane' implies a formal relationship and 'Hi Jane' reflects a more casual relationship. Sign-offs offer equally interpretive information, particularly the use of a signature 'block' or 'tag' which generally offers information about the person. A website, telephone number or famous quote may be offered. The signature block is interpreted as what the person holds dear to their public identity. Danet (2001) gives a fascinating analysis of the history of email and its place in letter writing. She defines two formats of email – the business template and the personal template, each with their own structures and forms of appropriate message writing. The business template – much like the writing of a letter on headed paper – has the formal approach between two professionals, using a greeting and a sign off that has been used in offices for decades. The personal template, which is much like a conversation between friends, has less formality and is more colloquial. (See the short examples in Figures 3.1 and 3.2.)

The approaches to writing emails in these examples are very different, and quite appropriately so. The first could be put on headed paper – it has a formal address in using 'Dear…', a formal sign-off in 'Sincerely', and factual information in between including a polite expression in anticipation of the meeting. The writer has also had the courtesy to CC a colleague into the mail, which pre-empts the need to forward it. The subject line includes the topic of the mail so that the importance of it can be recognized. The second email has little need for such formalities – it is from a friend who knows the recipient well enough not to have to address her formally, who greets her as if they had met in the street, and signs off with a shared salutation. The content, particularly the use of 'u' for 'you' and using lower case where capital letters would otherwise be appropriate from someone less well known, indicates a casual tone and a need for the speedy imparting of news. The subject line bears little relevance to the content, and yet shows that the sender has been thinking about getting together and wants to maintain that friendship, beyond the fact that they know they are meeting the following week.

Of course, analysis of emails such as the above is not done on a daily basis. What the recipient feels is a sense of the email overall – its tone, its content, and the emotion each one leaves us with. In contrast, consider the emails shown in Figures 3.3 and 3.4, one for business and one personal communication.

Subj: **Meeting – PM 2nd July**

Date: 6/18/09 9:00:15 AM GMT Daylight Time

From: Geoff@couns.org.uk

To: jane@email.co.uk

CC: peter@email.co.uk

Sent from the Internet (Details)

Dear Jane

Thanks for your message. I've put Wed 2nd July from 2pm in the diary.

I will start our session, but later in the afternoon I would like you to meet various other people in our organization that will also be involved in the project.

I look forward to meeting you and Peter soon.

Sincerely,

Geoff

FIGURE 3.1   EMAIL: MEETING – PM 2ND JULY

Subj: **It's been a while...**

Date: 6/17/09 10:03:29 AM GMT Daylight Time

From: joe@email.co.uk

To: Jane@email.co.uk

CC:

Sent from the Internet (Details)

(Continued)

FIGURE 3.2 (CONTINUED)

Hiya,

just in case u didn't know...

48 Thrills are playing The Cherry Tress, Norwood Junction this Saturday.

see u then? (If not, see u weds).

Cheers,

Joe

FIGURE 3.2 EMAIL: IT'S BEEN A WHILE...

Subj:	
Date:	6/18/03 9:00:15 AM GMT Daylight Time
From:	jkuu@aol.com
To:	Russ@email.co.uk
CC:	

Sent from the Internet (Details)

HI

my name is Jacob and I am a student at university. i found yr name whne looking at some researcch on the net and I was wondering if you could give me someinfo on online counseling for a project I'm doing'.

THANKS

FIGURE 3.3 EMAIL: INFORMAL EXAMPLE

The email in Figure 3.3 breaks several rules of Netiquette, and would therefore usually be considered not only rude by the recipient, but often downright insulting. The use of capital letters (HI, THANKS) is considered to be shouting when writing emails, there is no formal addressing of the recipient, and the lack of capital letters at the start of sentences and the failure to re-read the email before sending for spelling errors may indicate laziness and a lack of respect. There is no thought as to whether the recipient would have time or be willing to give information, and yet is thanked for it. Even if the recipient was willing to help, they would have no idea as to what sort of topic would be relevant. The spelling of 'counseling' would indicate that the sender is American, which would mean that different information may be appropriate were they to send it, but due to the typos throughout they could not be sure. There is also no subject line, which would mean that one may well delete it as spam (junk email) as it is from an unfamiliar address.

In contrast, in Figure 3.4, if you assume that Julie is Alison's closest friend, you can see how this formality is inappropriate and would leave Alison wondering whether Julie was upset with her, or alternatively whether she is cutting and pasting the same text to many people with differing levels of intimacy and therefore has not bothered to send a personal email, in which case Alison would be annoyed.

These examples are offered to demonstrate that what counts is the emotion that the recipient is left with rather than the specific content. Emails, mostly read on

Date:	6/18/09 9:00:15 AM GMT Daylight Time
From:	jules@email.com
To:	ally@email.co.uk
CC:	

Sent from the Internet (Details)

Dear Alison

I am planning to organize some sort of gathering at 8pm in The Antlers Pub, Plumstead, to celebrate my 30th birthday. I would be very pleased if you would attend.

Yours sincerely,

Julie

FIGURE 3.4   FORMAL EXAMPLE

screen and skimmed, rather than analyzed, can be extremely emotive, due to the interpretation placed upon them, the fantasy about the sender, and the transference of mood as discussed within theoretical considerations in Chapter 1.

But where do we place the therapeutic email in the hierarchy of writing? It is a professional transaction between client and practitioner, contracted and in many cases paid for as a business transaction. Yet the nature of the content of the emails is at the same time extremely personal. This is where the practitioner needs to develop a personal style of writing therapeutic emails, delivering a boundaried professional conversation that also conveys the core conditions of therapy.

Netiquette

When Tim Berners-Lee and the team at the Conseil Européenne pour la Recherche Nucléaire (CERN) completed the work on developing the World Wide Web, there was a dream of it mirroring 'the ways in which we work and play and socialize' (Berners-Lee, 1998). Yet the WWW actually went further than that in developing its own niceties and norms, and its own particular strand of deviance and actionable wording. The word 'Netiquette' – a combination of 'net' and 'etiquette' (Wikipedia, 2009) became the word for acceptable behavior when socializing and interacting in cyberspace. Deviance from the basic rules of polite respectful behavior is considered poor Netiquette, much as poor etiquette exists in society in the offline world.

Shea (1994) lists 10 rules of Netiquette, all applicable to the mental health professional that will be spending time in cyberspace as an online therapist. In development of a service, one will undoubtedly need to use forums for discussion with colleagues, find research papers, undertake online training courses and take part in live debates using chat rooms. Without knowledge of the basic rules of Netiquette, whether one's intensity of email use is defined as a newbie, casual, regular or avid user (Suler, 2003), time in cyberspace will be at the very least much more pleasant for knowing the rules, both personally and professionally. The 10 rules are summarized (using Shea's headings) as:

Rule 1: Remember the human

When sitting alone in one's office with one's computer using asynchronous methods of communication, it is easy to hear your own voice as you type, including all the tones and inflections that one would use in a conversation with someone. Therefore, as you write, you know what you mean and you assume that the person you are writing to will also know what you mean. This is not always the case; it is arguable that the recipient will hear their own voice when reading and give the text its own nuance and meaning. Therefore, it is essential to read each missive objectively, and ensure that the intended meaning will be understood by the person on the receiving end.

Rule 2: Adhere to the same standards of behavior online that you follow in the offline world

Just because cyberspace is a nebulous place it does not mean that there are different societal rules there. Ethical behavior is still paramount and illegal activities are still illegal. The well-documented rape in a multi-user dungeon (Dibbell, 1993), when a man took control of two females characters and made them perform sex acts on his own character, created huge debate over the Internet – no one doubted that it had happened (it was witnessed by the other game players), but the argument as to whether it constituted rape still rages in some places.

Rule 3: Know where you are in cyberspace

The specified standards or codes of conduct for interacting with others in cyberspace vary from domain to domain. Before joining any community, it is worth checking the rules of the site and lurking at the message boards before jumping in with your own opinions and thoughts. It can be likened to going to a party as a stranger and trying to take over the conversations – people will move away and ignore you at best, and take issue with you verbally at worst, with the potential for a 'flame war' to develop. Interaction in chat rooms also has the potential for causing offence – make sure you know the rules of each room, for example knowing where it is acceptable to swear, or to use euphemisms, or where to avoid that sort of language altogether.

Rule 4: Respect other people's time and bandwidth

Shea (1994) states that it is important to remember that you are not the center of cyberspace. Many people enjoy getting the rounds of Internet jokes that are rife, but a far greater amount of people do not. Responding to posts on email lists simply to state 'I agree' is a waste of time for every person who has to open the mail and then delete it just to know that you agree without having anything new to add to the conversation – you may well agree but most people won't care. This applies to copying lots of people in on an email: before clicking the send button, consider who actually needs to know the information.

Rule 5: Make yourself look good online

You will be judged by the quality of your writing in emails, forum postings and in chat rooms – that is, you will be judged by your appearance in text. This anonymity can be taken advantage of in many ways (which is why cyber-romances are so prevalent), and is why an understanding of the fantasy around the communicator, as discussed in Chapter 1, is so important.

Rule 6: Share expert knowledge

There was a debate amongst the members of the ISMHO as to if it may ever be appropriate to give away training materials developed by the experts among their number. The general consensus was that it was not appropriate, because the material was what the particular members used to make a living. It is, however, entirely appropriate (and usually expected) to post academic papers and writing online for dissemination to anyone who wants it. In a step further, it is also important, wherever possible and time permitting, to respond to polite requests for information or opinion (even Tim Berners-Lee took time to personally email one of the authors back about a request in 2003).

Rule 7: Help keep flame wars under control

Flame wars occur when someone has been intentionally rude or insulting and essentially wants to start a fight, or when the meaning and tone of a message has been misunderstood. They are an essential tradition of using the Internet, but can be very distressing when you are on the receiving end. In a conversation, you can clarify and apologize (if necessary) quite quickly and discreetly – in cyberspace, the insult and/or responze is there in text for everyone to see, which fans the flames of injustice and anger. Keeping flame wars under control is particularly important in a therapeutic group setting, but even more so in generic email lists and forums – every member can do their part to douse the flames.

Rule 8: Respect other people's privacy

Many individuals have access to back-ups of people's personal messages and data, especially in a work setting. Accessing such material is unacceptable. In addition, modern software allows you to know when another person is online. In this case, choosing to send an uninvited instant message to them should be done with care, with a polite request as to whether they are busy or have time for a conversation.

Rule 9: Don't abuse your power

This is more applicable to the online gaming world, where some individuals have been made wizards, and are given the power to facilitate the game – booting someone offline (kill or pin) in the face of unacceptable behavior for example. But even in less fantastic settings, such as message boards and forums, there is usually a facilitator with more power than other members to withhold messages and regulate membership. Such powers should not be abused, and this is relevant to the power dynamics of online therapy, for example where an in experienced therapist may be seen as expert beyond their actual competence.

Rule 10: Be forgiving of other people's mistakes

Once you have existed in cyberspace for some time, all these rules of Netiquette become second nature and you don't notice that you are a functioning member of a slightly different society. But Internet access is still growing worldwide, and new-bies arrive in cyberspace everyday, particularly with the advent of social network-ing sites. A polite word in someone's private inbox is all that is needed to point out where they are making mistakes – for instance, posting to a forum completely in capital letters (shouting). There is no need to point out to the entire membership of the forum that they have made a mistake. Another good rule of thumb is to rec-ognize your own mistakes and apologize for them – for instance, it is easy when talking quickly in chat rooms to press the Caps Lock button by mistake and inad-vertently find yourself shouting at people. In this case, a quick apology such as 'Soz, capslock' ('Sorry, I hit the Caps Lock key by mistake') is all that is needed to stop people complaining.

Netiquette is sometimes seen as something quirky about Internet communication, and therefore not to be taken seriously. It should be stressed, however, that it is Netiquette – not only knowledge of the rules but also the implementation of them as a norm – that is the backbone of being able to construct a therapeutic intervention. Typed text is so easily misconstrued, that a failing to use Netiquette can make a well-intentioned mis-sive into a minefield of insult and damaging words. To put this into a therapeutic con-text, the potential damage possible to a client who is well aware of the rules of Netiquette and reads your emails while applying them is huge. Whereas in face-to-face work the meaning of the words can be backed-up and conveyed by a tilt of the head, a smile and soft tone of voice, in cyberspace you have only the typed words, to which the recipient will attribute their own interpretation, whatever the intended meaning was. This is particularly important when interacting on group discussion boards, par-ticularly in a group therapeutic context, as is discussed further in Chapter 8.

To summarize, in personal emails, a relaxation of Netiquette is permissible. In business emails, it is not acceptable. In therapeutic emails, it can be potentially dangerous.

Emoticons

So how can we recreate the smile, the frown, the nod, the pauses, the gesticulations and everything else that goes into a conversation when sitting with a person face-to-face? One of the solutions to this when working only with the typed word is the use of what are known as emoticons – the creative use of keyboard characters to indicate to the other person what is happening at your end of the conversation. Emoticons are another facet of online communication that are often seen as some-how trite, and their application to therapy can provoke a reaction of horror that the range of human expression can be reduced to a kind of shorthand and yet still retain emotional impact. But emoticons are important in not only conveying emo-tion, but in helping reduce the amount of potential misunderstanding that typed text can carry.

Emoticons in their most well-known forms recreate three facial expressions – the smile, feeling sad, and the wink (see Box 3.1 for examples). The first two may seem obvious in indicating when you would smile at someone or show sadness when face-to-face, but the wink is often essential in online communication to show when you are not wholly serious or being ironic. Most western emoticons are recognized by inclining one's head to the left to see the characters as a face, but emoticons in Japan tend to be created horizontally (see highlighted in Box 3.1 cell). Online communicators develop or adopt their own preferred type of each and as communication software package version are developed, they tend to supply horizontal pictorial animated emoticons, for email, forums and chat.

BOX 3.1   EMOTICONS

Types of smileys	:)	:o)	(^_^)			
Types of sad faces	:(	:o(	:-(			
Types of winkeys	;)	;o)	;-)			

The use of emoticons in therapeutic communication needs to be led by the client – if they are familiar with using them and prefer their use to quickly indicate their emotions, then use of them by the therapist is entirely appropriate. It is also the therapist's responsibility to research emoticons that they are unfamiliar with, without using up valuable session time in asking what the client means by their keyboard strokes. Simple use of emoticons within a session can make a big difference in containing the client and making each participant's presence felt to their correspondent. If a client smiled at you in a face-to-face situation, it is unlikely that you would fail to return that smile.

Acronyms and abbreviations

Acronyms are also widely used in cyberspace communication. This is mostly true because the nature of online communication requires speed, as most people's typing ability is slower than that of their speech, and the lag between messages being sent and arriving slows down the conversation somewhat. Like emoticons, there are a few which are ubiquitous, and many cyberspace environments have their own individual preferences for their use. Using acronyms can be useful with someone familiar with them, but there are many that will only serve to confuse the reader. As an example, AFAIK (As Far As I Know) was used with many colleagues by one of the authors until she realized the majority had to email her for a translation. In client work, again it is the practitioner's responsibility to find the acronym on one of the many websites that list them before using up session time to ask for a translation.

As an example, the most widely used acronym is LOL, which stands for Laughing Out Loud (or Laugh Out Loud) and is used to indicate when you have found something amusing. There are many variations on this. For example, ROFL is Rolling On Floor Laughing, but within a client situation, LOL usually suffices since the material rarely gets that amusing (although it sometimes does). In addition, LOL is a bigger laugh than lol.

Enhancing text

The typed word read from a screen or indeed paper can seem very flat, with only the reader's interpretation of what is being said to bring it to life. As noted in Shea's (1994) rule 5 of Netiquette, you are how you type, and this includes a creative use of the tools at your fingertips (your keyboard and mouse) to enhance the text to imbue it with meaning, emphasis and emotion. In this way, the chances of misunderstanding are minimized and the text comes alive with your voice, increasing your presence and maintaining the therapeutic relationship as dynamic and interesting, rather than staid and depressingly dull.

The client who chooses online therapy will usually expect the text to be 'alive' because it is likely that they are familiar with Internet communication as a whole. However, each practitioner will develop their own style (which can sometimes fly in the face of Internet convention) to congruently reflect themselves in text. It has been reported, for example, that the use of lower case at the start of a sentence may reflect the way that the therapist speaks in face-to-face work, giving the text a poetic softness.

There are 10 basic guidelines to enhancing text well:

1. Use of capitalization

Using capital letters in text is considered to be shouting and is difficult (and unpleasant) to read. However, when working with emotive content capitals can be useful for emphasis in short bursts. Conversely, constructing a sentence completely in lower case can indicate laziness and a lack of respect for the client, as if you could not be bothered to re-read your words and correct grammatical errors.

For example, THIS SENTENCE IS PERCEIVED TO BE VERY LOUD AND RUDE. However, this sentence is MUCH better because the capital letters only emphasize the word 'much'. but this sentence shows laziness and is often considered disrespectful.

2. Emphasis

Originally, in the days before Windows and other user-friendly interfaces, the DOS text packages available contained no ability to emphasize words with bold text, underlining or italics. The convention then was to use either underscores or asterisks to show where a word was being emphasized, and this tradition remains in Internet communication today. Even with modern software tools for enhancing text, the translation between email packages can mean that the code used to enable this (HTML) gets substituted where previously there was bold or underlining, which can make text difficult to read.

For example:

This sentence is ★much ★ better.
This sentence is **much** better.
This sentence is much better.
This sentence is _ much _ better.

3. Use of exclamation marks

Many people tend to overuse exclamation marks to make a sentence amusing, and yet this can also make text difficult to read and irritate the recipient. A smiley or winkey emoticon does a much better job of indicating an exclamation, although one or two exclamation marks is usually acceptable. In therapeutic use, overuse of exclamation marks can often make serious text seem flippant.

For example, the text 'Maybe, in time, you could come to accept that everything you do doesn't have to be perfect!' can be rendered superficial by using too many exclamation marks thus: 'Maybe, in time, you could come to accept that everything you do doesn't have to be perfect!!!!!!!!!!'

4. Signature files

Signature files are a useful tool in business and social use of email, and are often inserted automatically into emails by the software package being used. The equivalent in chat is a pictorial icon by the screenname or login name you are using. For businesses they are the equivalent of a business card, and socially are a useful indication of a desire to show your personality across electronic channels (by inclusion of a favorite quote, for example). However, they should not be used within therapeutic emails and care should be taken to ensure they are not included in error. This is because the client is left with a sudden leap from your carefully constructed therapeutic style to either a business proposition or a fun flippant statement, often inappropriate in the face of the content of the mail.

5. Emotional bracketing and parenthetical use

As previously introduced, in cyberspace it is perfectly acceptable to hug one another, and this can be extended to therapeutic sessions without the dangers of giving a false erotic message that may be misinterpreted as such in a face-to-face session. Hugs are given by bracketing a person's name (or screen/login name), and clients often like the session to start or end with a hug as it increases the sense of presence, thus:

$$(((((((Jane)))))))$$

In addition, it is possible to give a group hug in a chatroom, thus:

$$(((((room)))))$$

As well as online hugs, there are many uses of emotional bracketing using other keyboard strokes that can enhance the text. For example:

'Maybe, in time, you could come to accept that everything you do doesn't have to be perfect <<wondering who told you that you always had to be>>'

and also to indicate a physical manifestation of an emotion away from the context of it:

'and then he left me anyway **[[sigh]]**'

6. CCing, BCCing and address books

One of the most dangerous facets of working online is the ability to send one email to many people, either with everyone's knowledge (ccing) or not (bccing). There is no situation in which replies to client email should be conveyed to someone else directly using these functions, even if using an online supervisor, since this would break confidentiality by communicating your client's email address (Anthony and Goss, 2009).

It is also good practice when replying to clients not to simply hit the 'reply' button, since this would preface your subject line with RE: which can sometimes be jarring for a client (giving a personal subject a business connotation). In using the narrative format for email work, it is sometimes useful for the previous correspondence to be contained in your email as reference, but this should always be cut and pasted into a new email where necessary.

The use of address books is also potentially dangerous. Firstly, the client's email address should not be contained within an address book because of reasons of confidentiality, but in addition it should be stressed to the client that your address should not be contained within theirs. Modern email software packages often autofill addresses and/or they can be selected from a list. With email addresses often being similar, the potential for your client to erroneously send a personal therapeutic email to, say, their boss or family member, is huge.

7. Greetings and sign-offs

These usually need, by their very nature, to be subject to the individual practitioner's style and preference, and often change over the course of a therapeutic relationship, becoming less formal as time goes on. Sign-offs in particular need focusing on, in considering how it will leave your client feeling. For example, a therapist used to ending face-to-face sessions with the words 'we'll have to leave it there', felt it entirely appropriate to translate to 'I'll have to leave it there' when signing off therapeutic emails. Closer examination, however, showed that those words could leave the client feeling as if they had taken up the practitioner's time when he should (or wanted to) be doing something else and that the client was a nuisance. This empathic consideration of the impact of your text on another person is essential in working online.

8. Subject lines

Some practitioners (Chechele and Stofle, 2003) prefer to use famous inspiring quotes as the subject line to their emails, others prefer a strong indication that the email is confidential in nature and therefore needs special attention. Not putting a subject at all (though easily done) is bad practice, indicating a lack of care, although many email softwares will alert you to this before the email is sent.

9. Paragraphing and definition of the conversation

When using a narrative style for working with a client, whether by email or forum, the body of it should always consist of many shorter paragraphs to give the client sizeable chunks to work with and this often helps them feel that they are managing the issues. Unbroken sections of text are difficult to read and feel chaotic and overwhelming to the client (who may be in a chaotic and overwhelming situation in their lives already).

When using a living document style (i.e inserting text within each other's emails) for working with a client, care should be taken to define the different parts of the progressing conversation by the use of different fonts or colors for each session. Fonts and colors should be chosen with an eye for echoing the tone of the words and content, rather than finding the strongest contrast. Living document email sessions tend to get unwieldy after four sessions.

10. The language of chat

Some chat or messaging programs have a limit to how much you can type before you have to hit the send button. Without indicating you have more to say, the client will think you have finished and start typing a response to find half way through that another sentence has appeared in the chat screen. Style of talking also varies from practitioner to practitioner – many use short sentences in order to minimize lag. Many more developed chat programmes indicate when the other party is typing, which is more convenient in a therapeutic setting as you can tell when to simply sit and wait for the words to come through, or where a more direct intervention is required if the conversation has halted.

Some examples of indicating you have more to say could be:

Therapist 20:   Maybe, in time, you could come to accept...
Therapist 20:   ... that everything you do doesn't have to be perfect.

Therapist 20:   Maybe, in time, you could come to accept (more)
Therapist 20:   that everything you do doesn't have to be perfect

Therapist 20:   Maybe, in time, you could come to accept that everything you
                  do doesn't have to be perfect (important question coming up!)
Therapist 20:   Do you think that could be possible?

As discussed in Chapter 2, screening the client for suitability to online work includes a determination of which method of delivery will most suit the client. In turn, as previously stated, a therapist may determine a preference for one method of delivery over another. Chechele and Stofle (2003) suggest that there seems to be a spectrum of closeness from email to chat to telephone and finally face-to-face counseling. This may be a generality as more and more therapists and clients are using methods of delivery interchangeably. One could posit that there is a more intimate quality to the communication when delivering counseling via Internet Relay Chat as opposed to email. While email may be compared to reading letters, the chat room may be seen as an actual virtual consultation room. The obvious difference between email as letter and chat as consultation room is that chat occurs synchronously while email is asynchronous. Just as in the face-to-face consultation room, the virtual consultation room must be void of distractions. The therapist creates an environment in which the work can take place without interruption and encourages the client to create a serene workspace as well. The difference between the face-to-face consultation room and the virtual consultation room is that the latter is co-created by the therapist and the client, each in their own space yet conjoined by the chat process (Nagel, 2008). This ease of use breaks down a certain formality that exists in face-to-face sessions and language use may become more casual as well, although rules of Netiquette still apply. As with email, Netiquette must be understood within the context of a chat session. Use of emoticons, acronyms and bracketing is as common in chat as within email. Several entire online dictionaries exist that give definitions of Internet acronyms and text messaging shorthand, providing instant access to a resource that can be used even in the midst of a chat session, for example, NetLingo, dubbed 'the semantics storehouse of cyberspace' (Netlingo, 2001).

CONCLUSION

Potential misunderstandings most likely to occur during online text-based therapy include the following:

- Cues are different. As previously discussed, the lack of visual and/or auditory cues changes the nature of the delivery.
- Time shifting occurs and depending on typing skills, various platform and chat program differences, clients or therapists might interpret a quick or slow response as meaningful in some way, possibly making inferences unnecessarily.
- Messages, both email and chat can be lost in cyberspace due to program or platform malfunction.
- Cultural issues can pose problems if the therapist is not aware of the cultural differences from the onset of therapy.
- The client may drop out of treatment due to dissatisfaction. The key is to determine if the dissatisfaction was caused by technology, e.g. the method in which the counseling was delivered, or the therapy itself, or whether circumstances have changed for the client so that they consider therapy no longer necessary.

At this point, we have developed an understanding of the culture of cyberspace, with all of its nuances and characteristics, via discussion of theoretical aspects of the work, the essential skills of online work, and the techniques involved in the use of text online. In the next chapter we will cover the ethical considerations inherent in online work and introduce a new framework for the use of technology in mental health.

REFERENCES

Anthony, K. and Goss, S. (2009) *Guidelines for Online Counselling and Psychotherapy, Including Guidelines for Online Supervision, 3rd edition*. Lutterworth: BACP.

Berners-Lee, T. (1998) 'The World Wide Web: A Very Short Personal History', in *W3C World Wide Web Consortium*. Available at www.w3.org/people/berners-lee/shorthistory. html [accessed 3 April 2009].

Chechele, P. and Stofle, G. (2003) 'Individual Therapy Online via Email and Internet Relay Chat', in S. Goss and K. Anthony (eds), *Technology in Counselling and Psychotherapy: A Practitioner's Guide*. Basingstoke: Palgrave Macmillan.

Danet, B. (2001) *Cyberpl@y*. Oxford: Berg.

Dibbell, J. (1993) 'A Rape in Cyberspace', in *The Village Voice,* December 21: 36–42.

Krause, S. (2008) 'Thinking Outside the In-box: From Address to Zinger, Email Delivers Special Challenges', in *Psychology Today*, 25 August, Article ID: 4636. Available at www.psychology today.com/articles/pto-20080718-000004.html [accessed 7 April 2009].

Nagel, D.M. (2008) 'Filling the Void in the Virtual Consultation Room', in *Voices: the Art and Science of Psychotherapy*, 44(1): 98–101.

Netlingo (2001) 'An Interview with Erin Jansen "Author & Publisher"', in *Netlingo*. Available at www.netlingo.com/press/about-netlingo.php [accessed 7 April 2009].

Shea, V. (1994) *Netiquette*. San Francisco: Albion Books.

Suler, J. (2003) 'E-Mail Communication and Relationships', in *The Psychology of Cyberspace*. Available at www-usr.rider.edu/~suler/psycyber/emailrel.html#intensity [accessed 7 April 2009].

Suler, J. (2004) 'The Psychology of Text Relationships', in R. Kraus, J. Zack and G. Striker (eds), *Online Counseling: A Manual for Mental Health Professionals*. London: Elsevier Academic Press.

Wikipedia (2009) 'Netiquette', in *Wikipedia, The Free Enclyclopedia*. Available at http://en.wikipedia.org/wiki/Netiquette [accessed 7 April 2009].

4
ETHICAL CONSIDERATIONS

INTRODUCTION

How to work ethically online has been the topic of much debate across the globe, and quite rightly so. The advent of the Internet and working with text electronically exploded many of the safe environments that traditionally we were familiar with working face-to-face. Where there were previously four walls, a ceiling and floor, and two chairs within which to contain the therapeutic relationship, there is now an ephemeral space with no physical limits and many unknown technological factors, such as where on a hard drive material actually goes as it is stored, to contend with. Even once there were clear answers to the argument that it 'isn't really therapy, is it?' the ethical considerations that needed to be considered seemed insurmountable in the face of communication that could be done globally and that transcended time differences and cultures.

Working ethically online should be paramount for any practitioner, regardless of which modality they are using, just as is the case face-to-face. Whatever code of ethics a practitioner adheres to, they should stand as a basic framework for working online. There are many issues that need special attention when working with communication over the Internet, and many of these are still being discovered and worked out all over the world. Evidence-based practice was unfeasible when Internet therapy was demanded by the client base, and the pioneers of the method were left to work out not only how to do it, but how to do it ethically, before any empirical research was available. Many of the ethical issues that were relevant back in the mid 1990s, and even some from the mid 2000s, are now irrelevant, mostly because technological applications are developed and change so quickly. For example, encryption packages are far superior now to those that were available at the time, and therefore cost-effective options exist that allow for much more secure communication.

This chapter is offered to introduce the basic ethical principles that should be considered before setting up an online service. Many of the issues within this chapter still don't have a definitive answer or a general consensus as to what is regarded as right globally. Practitioners working online tend to find their own level of what they feel is right or wrong when working online – for instance, many online therapists find working with Internet Relay Chat uncomfortable and can't correlate it to being a natural conversation, and therefore exclude it from their online services. This is a good instance of working ethically online – it is up to the therapist to take account of how working with text and the modality impacts on their ethical stance, and take action accordingly, just as with regard to the their determining which method of text-based therapy delivery is the best fit for them.

Obviously, there are not just differing guidelines between different countries; there are also differing guidelines between organizations within those countries. It is also the case that the different organizations base their guidelines upon their preferred theoretical orientation, but an examination at that level is not within the remit of this chapter. Instead, we will concentrate on the main themes that are common to most of the developed and published guidelines and ethical statements available to the profession worldwide by some of the larger associations and professional bodies. We will pay particular attention to what is probably the most comprehensive document on the subject which was published by the British Association for Counselling and Psychotherapy in 2001 (Goss et al., 2001) – updated in 2005, when the first Guidelines for online supervision were introduced (Anthony and Jamieson, 2005), and again in 2009 with additional information in light of the surge of social networking sites and other community-based websites and including an extended single case study (Anthony and Goss, 2009).

Guidelines and suggested principles started to appear a couple of years after the first online services were offered, by organizations such as the ISMHO in 1997 (ISMHO, 2000), the National Board for Certified Counselors (Morrissey, 1997) and the American Counseling Association (ACA, 1999). In addition, in 1999, Kraus and others developed an ethics code for organizations and individual practitioners who practice online in the field of health care (Kraus, et al., 1999). To date, many mental health disciplines have revised or developed Codes of Ethics that incorporate the use of technology. A comprehensive and up-to-date list of guidelines and ethical codes relevant to mental health and technology is available in one resource online; the Online Therapy Institute's Wiki (Anthony and Nagel, 2009) is open to anyone who wishes to join and update information related to ethics and law within his or her particular geographic region.

To gain a comprehensive spread of these Guidelines and suggested principles, the following discussion takes account of the content of each of these original five main publications. It should be noted that revised and updated versions of the ACA Code of Ethics and BACP Guidelines have been issued in subsequent years, and reflect a much higher standard of care than when first published.

INFORMED CONSENT

Informed consent is probably the most central ethical issue that professionals have considered in Guideline development. As online therapy came about ahead of any proper exploration of the advantages and disadvantages inherent in using the Internet for mental health, practitioners could only rely on ensuring that they gave the client as much information as possible about the potential benefits and risks and making sure the client had enough knowledge about them to decide whether the modality would be of benefit to them and before consenting to taking part. Therefore, every practitioner who practises online should have a page on their site dedicated to informing the client about topics such as the process of the therapy, what to expect, alternative avenues of help and the safeguards in place against the risks of having online therapy. In the initial course of intake, the informed consent should be acknowledged as read and understood by the client. This can occur via a checked box on the website or Intake Questionnaire or other verifiable process.

PRACTITIONER COMPETENCE

Experience

As previously stated, it is generally accepted that online therapy is not appropriate for the novice or inexperienced practitioner. Although it is impossible to state a base level for appropriate qualifications due to the differences in training and accreditation/licensing from country to country, it should be recognized that competence in one medium (i.e. face-to-face) does not necessarily translate into being competent in online work. Many practitioners will never be comfortable working without the physical presence, and many practitioners will never be comfortable working with technology. In addition, there will always be models of therapy that are less suited to being adapted from face-to-face work to text. Guidelines also state as a rule of thumb that if you are not qualified to work with a particular client group offline, then it should be assumed that you are not qualified to work with them online.

Practitioners also need to consider the impact that working online will have on the other modalities they employ – for example, online work is often more direct and dynamic than working face-to-face because of having to be explicit about interpretations and emotions to avoid miscommunication, and therapists may find that this facet of online communication gets carried into their face-to-face work. There may also be frustration when offline clients have difficulty in admitting to certain thoughts and feelings that would be offered much sooner when working at a distance from the therapist.

Training

Training for transferring from face-to-face work to working with text has been available since around the turn of the millennium, and more and more practitioners are undertaking training that encompasses the practical, theoretical and ethical discussions that surround this modality (see Chapter 7). Working online is a specialist area, and one that requires additional skills, training and experience. Unfortunately – and just as in the traditional modalities, particularly in the UK as well as other parts of the world – anyone can set themselves up as an online therapist, and regulation of this type of work still eludes us.

Computer skills

The ability to type quickly and accurately is less of an issue in email or forum work, but in Interact Relay Chat (IRC) it should be considered essential if this is not to get in the way of the therapeutic process. Because of the time it takes to transmit messages back and forth across the Internet ('lag'), it can be frustrating for the client to have to cope with that and also a slow typing therapist, particularly if they are paying for the session.

It is not necessary to know how to build a computer or write programs to be a competent online therapist, but the practitioner's knowledge of how their operating system works, how their communication system works (for both the email 'client' and their ISP), and the benefits and limitations of any software used, should be thorough. In addition, although some of the more advanced aspects of cyberspace (blogging and virtual reality sites, for example) may never be used by the practitioner, there should be a good understanding of what they are and why people use them.

Under this heading, we should also consider the use and knowledge of firewalls, viruses and similar destructive programs, and the appropriate use of attachments. It is good practice not to open any files received where you do not know or cannot trust the source, even sometimes from a client or potential client, and it is important that the practitioner has a good, frequently updated (at least once every two weeks) anti-virus software programme. The ability to spot suspect files is useful and should not be underestimated, as well as keeping up with news of new viruses, worms or Trojan Horses. This seems a glib point, but with viruses that send themselves to people in your address book automatically, the potential of the practitioner sending a virus to a client could have damaging effects, both practically and emotionally.

Proper firewall installation is a must on any computer that uses the Internet. Basic programs, such as Zone Alarm (ZoneAlarm, 2009), are free and easily downloadable. Another aspect of working in cyberspace is an awareness of hoax emails and scams. Apart from the obvious scams such as the Nigerian 419 emails, there are often hoaxes that tell you a file on your drive is a virus and that you must delete it for your data and hardware to be safe. Still, with the advent of social networking, therapists must stay informed about new and potentially harmful viruses. While anti-virus programs are becoming more and more reliable, it is still advised that therapists are careful about clicking on links or downloading files and pictures from a social networking site, even those that appear to be from a known person.

Verification of qualifications

All guidelines to online work state methods by which the client can verify that the therapist is who they say they are (although pseudonyms are often appropriate online, in this case the full name of the therapist should be used), and can access information about what degrees or diplomas are held along with pertinent information about additional qualifications and training. Further information should include the details, along with a link and phone number, of the practitioner's professional body and what the procedure is in the event of a complaint. Additionally, the client has to be able to assess the counselor's personality and methods of working, and should be able to do so from the website (which is the first test of whether one can convey oneself online adequately enough to be able to work therapeutically with another person).

CLIENT INCLUSION AND EXCLUSION

The debate about which client groups are suitable for working online, and which are not, still rages across the globe. It is true that there are some psychiatric conditions that should be excluded from working online, but these tend to be those that need more medical input than just receiving counseling or psychotherapy. There are many client groups that seem to indicate a need for exclusion from working over the Internet, and yet work with these groups is not only possible, but also very successful. Barak (2007) uses email with schizophrenic patients as a communication tool in the event of a psychiatric breakdown between face-to-face appointments. The Samaritans email service receives a huge number of emails per 24 hours from people with suicidal ideation. The Center for BrainHealth, University of Texas, Dallas, works online with people who have been diagnosed with Asperger's syndrome, schizophrenia and ADHD (Nagel, 2009). While the intervention occurs in a virtual world setting, chat and messaging is used and available within the platform.

Other conditions that are debatable as to whether or not they are suitable for online work are those related to addictions to alcohol or drugs (since you cannot see whether they are under the influence of the drug at the time). Many face-to-face practitioners exclude clients from sessions if they are under the influence of alcohol or drugs, in which case the online client contract should specify this policy. However, this would be difficult to assess when working with email (although emails written under the influence of alcohol in particular tend to be entirely disinhibited and often very long), and also difficult to assess in a chat room, although a change in typing accuracy may indicate that the client may be drunk or high. But to accuse an addicted client of this in an online session is likely to be dangerous to their state of mind, whether accurate or not, and the online practitioner must work with whatever level of communication is possible without judging the client. If the client openly admits to being under the influence at the time of the session then the therapist can use his or her best clinical judgement as to whether to continue with the session. The other option when working with substance abusers is to add a video component to the therapy process. Egetgoing (eGetgoing, 2009) is an online treatment facility based in the United States that has achieved national accreditation for their addiction programs, which uses a combination of distance technologies to facilitate therapy.

Gary Stofle (2001) provides a useful 'level of care' table to show what types of issue and client mental states are appropriate for online work, and which are more suited to face-to-face or hospital treatment. He draws the line at clients who have seriously disordered thinking and who are eligible for medication and day patient status. This shows the importance of a good intake process for potential online clients which asks for information such as what previous methods of help and support have been sought out and what medication the client is taking or has been prescribed previously. The client can, of course, give false information in filling out intake and assessment forms, but if the practitioner can demonstrate an ethical and solid level of attempting to gain a whole picture of the client's mental health, then this is sufficient to make an informed decision as to whether online work is suitable for them. This chapter provides more discussion about the assessment and intake procedure, as well as what happens when it becomes clear that a client should not be receiving online assistance after all.

Cultural issues

The World Wide Web, by its very definition, transcends cultural barriers and we must therefore consider carefully what issues this throws up for practitioners. Cross-cultural therapy need not be problematic in the world of face-to-face practice, and this applies just as well when working over the Internet. The important point to consider in this context, however, is that it is likely to occur on a much more regular basis where geographical boundaries are rendered unimportant. Even the one boundary that remains in cyberspace – that of differing time zones – is irrelevant in the case of working with email (and is often surmountable when working with Internet Relay Chat).

A certain level of cultural sensitivity is required when you are working with a client in any modality of therapy, and it is unlikely that a full level of cultural understanding is likely if it is not one's own. However, important clues are given in the client's location and description of themselves, which will allow for research to be done to ensure that assumptions are not made – particularly with regard to issues such as sexuality, religious practice and abortion rights. It should be remembered that practitioners have a responsibility to research different cultures as they occur in client work, via the web, and that this is a remarkably simple process using search engines and websites which originate from the culture the client is living in.

Age of client

Online work seems particularly suited to younger people, who have grown up being familiar with the Internet and other technological developments. Practitioners who wish to offer a service to potential clients who are considered a minor in any particular country need to carefully consider what additional safeguards they can offer the client and where their duty lies in informing a parent, guardian, or other responsible person. For private practitioners, whether individual or organizational, it should be noted that proof of adult status should not necessarily be indicated by use of a credit card or Internet paying account, such as PayPal. If a minor is using a family computer, additional confidentiality structures may be appropriate.

Working with young children over the Internet can be very fulfilling when it comes to methods involving practical materials, such as art therapy. By using computer tools such as painting software and transmitting these over the Internet to the qualified practitioner, a lot of work can be achieved with minors who have little other access to sources of help. Malchiodi (2000) discusses these methods thoroughly in her book on art therapy and computer technology. Issues such as the potential of using virtual reality environments with minors to explore feelings and emotions are discussed in Chapter 9.

PRACTICAL ISSUES REFLECTING BEST PRACTICE

Many ethical considerations have been addressed and offered thus far. Establishing the best standard of care at all times and always protecting client information is of utmost importance to the online therapist. Additional points are offered here that summarize the varying and necessary components of practicing confidentially (Nagel and Anthony, 2009a).

- Are computer screens visible to clients or others who should not have access to confidential information?
- Are computers password protected?
- Is the facsimile machine located securely?
- Is using a mobile phone to discuss confidential information practical and/or safe?
- Is the practitioner using unencrypted email to disseminate confidential information?
- Is the practitioner using unencrypted instant messaging or chat programs such as Yahoo or AOL?

CONCLUSION AND INTRODUCTION TO THE OTI ETHICAL FRAMEWORK

The initial discussions in this chapter thus far offer a generic set of principles for working online – that is, they are of importance to online practitioners globally. What is important to note is that a global ethical framework now exists and it is necessary for online therapy to finally be embraced. Ideally, this framework should exist alongside a global registry of trained, ethically practicing Internet therapists. If cyberspace is an environment that transcends global boundaries, then a view that international guidelines should be possible is entirely appropriate and should be encouraged.

The summary of the aforementioned developed guidelines and codes provides collectively a set of indications for best practice. What has been lacking is one framework that draws these guidelines and codes together. There now exists such a framework, developed by the authors of this book, which recognizes both fluid and rigid expectations of practitioners, organizations and regions around the globe. The Online Therapy Institute's Ethical Framework for the Use of Technology in Mental Health (Nagel and Anthony, 2009b) provides the most thorough standard of care model currently available to mental health practitioners. This ethical framework offers the basics of the original codes and guidelines of the BACP, ACA, NBCC, ISMHO and Ethics Code, incorporating additions that appear in the revised ACA Code of Ethics and the 2nd and 3rd editions of the BACP guidelines.

ETHICAL FRAMEWORK FOR THE USE OF TECHNOLOGY IN MENTAL HEALTH

A competent practitioner working online will always adhere *at least* to the following minimum standards and practices in order to be considered to be working in an ethical manner.

PRACTITIONERS HAVE A SUFFICIENT UNDERSTANDING OF TECHNOLOGY

Technology basics are required for practitioners who choose to deliver therapeutic services via technology. Practitioners will possess a basic understanding of technology as the technology relates to delivery of services

- **Encryption**: Practitioners understand how to access encrypted services to store records and deliver communication. Records storage can be hosted on a secure server with a third-party, stored on the practitioner's hard drive utilizing encrypted folders or stored on an external drive that is safely stored.
- **Backup Systems**: Records and data that are stored on the practitioner's hard drive are backed up either to an external drive or remotely via the Internet.
- **Password Protection**: Practitioners take further steps to ensure confidentiality of therapeutic communication and other materials by password protecting the computer, drives and stored files or communication websites.
- **Firewalls**: Practitioners utilize firewall protection externally or through web-based programs.
- **Virus Protection**: Practitioners protect work computers from viruses that can be received from or transmitted to others, including clients.
- **Hardware**: Practitioners understand the basic running platform of the work computer and know whether or not a client's hardware/platform is compatible with any communication programs the practitioner uses.
- **Software**: Practitioners know how to download software and assist clients with the same when necessary to the delivery of services.
- **Third-party Services**: Practitioners utilize third-party services that offer an address and phone number so that contact is possible via means other than email. This offers a modicum of trust in the third-party utilized for such services as backup, storage, virus protection and communication.

PRACTITIONERS WORK WITHIN THEIR SCOPE OF PRACTICE

Scope of Practice indicates the specific area in which a practitioner may practice. Scope of Practice in many geographic areas also defines where a practitioner

(Continued)

(Continued)

may practice; whether the practitioner may practice across various geographical boundaries and within what parameters a practitioner may practice. Practitioners also follow local and regional laws and codes of ethics as applicable.

- Understanding of boundaries and limitations of one's specific discipline: Practitioners understand which assessments and interventions are allowed within their specific discipline. For instance, helping professionals who assist with career issues and have no training generally do not provide psychotherapy services.
- Understanding of specific laws or ethics within one's own discipline or geographic location: Practitioners understand the limits set forth by laws or ethics within the applicable geographic location. For instance, in the United States, Licensed Professional Counselors cannot call themselves Psychologists, and in the UK the term 'Chartered Psychologist' is reserved by law for use only by those with proper recognition from the appropriate authorities. Certain states dictate what a practitioner can be called due to the implementation of Title laws. Practice laws may prevent a licensed practitioner from interpreting certain personality tests in one state, yet the same practice may be accepted under Practice law in another state.
- Respect for the specific laws of a potential client's geographic location: Practitioners understand that different geographic regions may offer additional limits to practice, particularly with regard to jurisdiction. For instance, a counselor in the UK should be cognizant of the laws of a client who resides in a U.S. state such as California, in which the law prohibits consumers residing in California from engaging in counseling from a practitioner who is not licensed in California.

PRACTITIONERS SEEK OUT TRAINING, KNOWLEDGE AND SUPERVISION

Training, knowledge and supervision regarding mental health and technology is paramount to delivering a standard of care that is considered 'best practice' within one's geographic region and within a global context. Practitioners are encouraged to demonstrate proficiency and competency through formal specialist training for online work, books, peer-reviewed literature and popular media. Clinical and/or peer supervision and support are mandated for practitioners who cannot practice independently within a geographic region and is highly recommended for all practitioners.

- **Formal Training**: Practitioners seek out sufficient formal training whenever possible through college, university or private settings. Formal training is displayed on the practitioner's website.
- **Informal Training**: Practitioners seek out continuing education and professional development and conferences, conventions and workshops.
- **Books:** Practitioners read books written by the general public and professionals.
- **Peer-reviewed Literature**: Practitioners read peer-reviewed literature that includes the latest theories and research.

- **Popular Media**: Practitioners are informed through popular media such as magazines, newspapers, social networking sites, websites, television and movies and understand the impact of mental health and technology on the popular culture.
- **Clinical/Peer Supervision**: Practitioners seek clinical supervision whenever the practitioner cannot practice independently within his or her geographic location. Clinical and/or peer supervision is sought by all practitioners who deliver services via technology. Clinical and peer supervision is delivered either face-to-face or via encrypted methods.

Example Topics of study related to Training, Knowledge and Supervision (not an exhaustive list):

- Online Therapy
- Online Clinical Supervision
- Online Peer Supervision
- Avatar Therapy
- Cyberpsychology
- Text-based Therapy
- Telehealth
- Behavioral Telehealth
- Telepsychiatry
- Internet Addictions
- Social Media
- Mixed Reality
- Online Relationships
- Second Life
- Online Peer Support
- SMS Text Messaging
- Virtual Worlds
- Virtual Reality
- Mental Health and Technology

PRACTITIONERS DISPLAY PERTINENT AND NECESSARY INFORMATION ON WEBSITES

Websites provide access to information for the general public, potential clients, clients and other professionals.

- **Crisis Intervention Information**: People may surf the internet seeking immediate help. Practitioners display crisis intervention information on the home page. Practitioners understand that people in crisis may visit the website from anywhere in the world.

(Continued)

(Continued)

Offering global resources such as Befriender's International or The Samaritans is the best course of action.

- **Practitioner Contact Information**: Practitioners offer contact information that includes email, post address and a telephone or VOIP number. While it is not recommended that post addresses reflect the practitioner's home location, clients should have a post address for formal correspondence related to redress, subpoenas or other mailings requiring a signature of receipt. Practitioners state the amount of time an individual may wait for a reply to email or voice mail. Best practice indicates a maximum of two business days for therapeutic inquiries.

- **Practitioner Education, License and/or Certification Information**: Practitioners list degrees, licenses and/or certifications as well as corresponding numbers. If the license, certification board, or professional body offers a website that allows the general public to verify information on a particular practitioner the license and certification listings should link directly to those verifying body websites. Practitioners consider listing other formal education such as college or university courses, online continuing education and professional development courses, and conference/convention attendance directly related to mental health and technology.

- **Terms of Use and Privacy Policy**: Terms of Use, often all or in part, synonymous with a practitioner's informed consent, is available on the website either as a page on the website or a downloadable document. The practitioner's privacy policy is also available in the same way and offers information about if or how email addresses, credit card information and client records are used, shared or stored. Practitioners must ensure that they comply with the requirements of the Data Protection Act and other aspects of applicable law, and in the United States, practitioners display the Notice of Privacy Practices to indicate compliance with HIPAA. Applicable information regarding privacy and confidentiality that are required for patient consent in the geographic location of the practitioner should be posted on the website as well.

- **Encrypted Transmission of Therapeutic and Payment Information**: Practitioners offer secure and encrypted means of therapeutic communication and payment transactions. Email and Chat programmes whether embedded within the practitioner site (private practice or e-clinic) or utilizing 3rd party platforms such as Hushmail or Cryptoheaven are explained on the website. Payment methods are explained as well through merchant information or information provided by the practitioner.

PRACTITIONERS CONDUCT AN INITIAL INTAKE AND SCREENING PROCESS

The initial screening and intake process begins with the potential client's first contact. The practitioner implements formal and informal measures for screening a client's suitability for delivery of mental health services via technology.

- **Client's Technology Skills**: Practitioners screen potential client's use of technology through questions at the outset. Questions include but are not limited to an inquiry about the client's experience with online culture e.g. email, chat rooms, forums, social networks, instant messaging and online purchasing, mobile texting, VOIP or telephones. Practitioners ensure that the client's platform is compatible with the varying programmes and platforms the practitioner may utilize during the course of therapy.
- **Client's Language Skills**: Practitioners screen for language skills from the initial contact through the first few exchanges. Assessing for language barriers, reading and comprehension skills as well as cultural differences is part of the screening process. Text-based therapy may also involve screening for keyboarding proficiency.
- **Presenting Issue, Client Identity and Clinical Concerns**: Practitioners screen to ensure the presenting issue is within the scope of practice and knowledge base of the practitioner. Screening around issues of suicidality, homicidality and immediate crisis are formally addressed through an intake questionnaire or first exchange. Practitioners incorporate a mechanism for verifying identity of clients by asking for a formal identification number such as Driver's License or other satisfactory method. The client must not be anonymous, offering at a minimum: first and last name, home address and phone number for emergency contact. Minors must be identified through parental consent. If client identity is not required, such as is the case with crisis hotlines and triage settings, limitations of the service are stated clearly. Other concerns regarding mental stability are addressed – e.g. client currently hallucinating or delusional or actively using drugs and alcohol to an extent that insight-oriented interventions would not be suitable, and finally any other medical or physical issues that might impede the intervention or require a different method of delivery, e.g. disability that impairs typing, rendering a chat exchange cost-prohibitive. Any assessment instrumentals that are utilized should be approved for online or computer-assisted use according to the test author/publisher.

PRACTITIONERS OFFER AN INFORMED CONSENT PROCESS

The Informed Consent process begins when the client contemplates accessing services. Therefore, clear and precise information is accessible via the practitioner's website. The Informed Consent process includes a formal acknowledgement from the client to the practitioner. This acknowledgement is received via encrypted or secure methods. Informed Consent content is revisited during the course of therapy as necessary and beneficial.

The following topics are addressed within Informed Consent:

- **Possible Advantages and Disadvantages of Online Therapy**: Information is disseminated about the pros and cons of online therapy including such disadvantages

(Continued)

(Continued)

as lack of visual and auditory cues and the limitations of confidentiality via technology, and advantages that include easy scheduling, time management and a no need to incur transportation costs.

Confidentiality and Technology

- **Encryption**: An explanation about the use of encryption for therapeutic exchanges and lack of encryption if/when unencrypted methods (standard email, forum posts, mobile telephone, SMS texting, social networking) are used for issues such as appointment changes and cancellations.
- **Therapist as Owner of the Record**: Unless otherwise specified through law in the practitioner's geographic location, the therapist remains the owner of the therapeutic record including all transcripts, notes and emails. The client is informed that posting direct information about the therapist or verbatim information from sessions is prohibited.
- **File Storage Procedures**: The client is informed about how records are stored (web-based, third party or hard-drive/external drive) and for how long the records are maintained. All procedures conform to the standards laid down in applicable law and as required by any relevant authority (such as professional body) and, at least, include encryption and password protection and a commitment to destroy all records after a given period as required by law/regulation/best practice.
- **Privacy Policy**: The practitioner's privacy policy is also included in the Informed Consent process including information about how email addresses, credit card information and client records are used, shared or stored. In the United States, practitioners must include the Notice of Privacy Practices to indicate compliance with HIPAA. Applicable information regarding privacy and confidentiality that are required for patient consent in the geographic location of the practitioner are included in the Informed Consent process.

Other Informed Consent Issues

- **Practitioner's Geographical Jurisdiction**: The physical location of the practitioner is offered in the Informed Consent and if the practitioner is licensed within a specific jurisdiction, the Informed Consent states client understands services are rendered under the laws or jurisdiction of the relevant country, state or region.
- **How to Proceed during a Technology Breakdown**: The client is informed about how to proceed if a technology breakdown occurs during a session, e.g. 'If we disconnect, try to reconnect within 10 minutes. If reconnection is not possible, email or call to reschedule an appointment.'
- **Emergency Contact**: Practitioners offer specific information about who to contact in case of an emergency and set specific rules about emergency emails that the

practitioner may not be privy to (e.g. suicidal emails in the middle of the night, threatening posts on a support forum). Practitioners research local resources within the client's geographic area as emergency backup resources.

- **Cultural Specifics that May Impact Treatment**: Practitioners discuss varying time zones, cultural differences and language barriers that may impact the delivery of services. Practitioners should also ensure at or prior to the start of therapy, that the client's expectations of the service being offered (such as the meaning of the term 'counseling' etc.) is sufficiently close to their own understanding and should take into account that different cultures around the world can have very different understandings of these matters.
- **Dual Relationships**: Practitioners discuss with clients the expected boundaries and expectations about forming relationships online. Practitioners inform clients that any requests for 'friendship', business contacts, direct or @replies, blog responses or requests for a blog response within social media sites will be ignored to preserve the integrity of the therapeutic relationship and protect confidentiality. If the client has not been formally informed of these boundaries prior to the practitioner receiving the request, the practitioner will ignore the request via the social media site and explain why in subsequent interaction with the client.
- **Insurance, Subsidy or Reimbursement Information**: If the client resides in a geographic area that generally accepts insurance or other forms of reimbursement for therapy services, the practitioner informs the client of this information. Conversely, services delivered via technologies that are not covered at all or at the same rate, the practitioner informs the client of this information also.

Thus far we have discussed the theoretical, skilful, practical and ethical aspects of online therapy. The next chapter will address the business aspects of developing an online service.

REFERENCES

American Counseling Association (ACA) (1999) 'Ethical Standards for Internet Online Counseling'. Available at www.angelfire.com/co2/counseling/ethical.html [accessed 7 April 2009].

Anthony, K. and Goss, S. (2009) Guidelines for *Online Counselling and Psychotherapy, Including Guidelines for Online Supervision, 3rd edition*. Lutterworth: BACP.

Anthony, K. and Jamieson, A. (2005) *Guidelines for Online Counselling and Psychotherapy, Including Guidelines for Online Supervision, (2nd edition)*. Lutterworth: BACP.

Anthony, K. and Nagel, D.M. (2009) 'Online Therapy Wiki', in *Online Therapy Institute*. Available at www.onlinetherapy.wikispaces.com [accessed 9 April 2009].

Barak, A. (2007) 'Emotional Support and Suicide Prevention through the Internet: A Field Project Report', in *Computers in Human Behavior*, 23(2): 971–84.

eGetgoing (2009) 'Online Group Therapy – Anonymous, Convenient, Affordable', in *eGetgoing*. Available at www.egetgoing.com/ [accessed 8 April 2009].

Goss, S., Anthony, K., Jamieson, A. and Palmer, S. (2001) *Guidelines for Online Counselling and Psychotherapy*. Rugby: BACP.

ISMHO (2000) 'Suggested Principles for the Online Provision of Mental Health Services', in *ISMHO*. Available at www.ismho.org/suggestions.asp [accessed 7 April 2009].

Kraus, R, Stricker, G., Hillowe, B. and Hall, J. (1999) 'Guidelines for Mental Health and Healthcare Practice Online', in *EthicsCode.com*. Available at www.ethicscode.com [accessed 8 April 2009].

Malchiodi, C. (2000) *Art Therapy and Computer Technology*. London: Jessica Kingsley Publishers Ltd.

Morrissey, M. (1997) 'NBCC WebCounseling Standards Unleash Intense Debate', in *Counseling Today*, 40(5): 6(8): 12.

Nagel, D.M. (2009) 'People with Asperger's Syndrome Learn Social Skills in Second Life', in *Telehealth World*, 2(1): 1–8.

Nagel, D.M. and Anthony, K. (2009a) 'Forensic Mental Health and Technology: Risk Management Strategies for the Practitioner', in *The Forensic Examiner*, 18(1): 62–4.

Nagel, D.M. and Anthony, K. (2009b) 'Ethical Framework', in *Online Therapy Institute*. Available at www.onlinetherapyinstitute.com/id43.html [accessed 8 April 2009].

Stofle, G. (2001) *Choosing an Online Therapist*. Harrisburg PA: White Hat Communications.

ZoneAlarm (2009) 'ZoneAlarm for your Home and Small Business', in *ZoneAlarm*. Available at www.zonealarm.com [accessed 8 April 2009].

5
THE BUSINESS OF
ONLINE THERAPY

INTRODUCTION

Up to this point, we have discussed the theory, the skill and the ethics of online therapy. In this chapter, we will talk about how to turn abstract concepts into a successful service people will want to access and use. We begin with a brief look at a historical timeline of online therapy.

The history of online therapy can be summarized in a few paragraphs, beginning with a look at some of the early computer-mediated communication programs. Grohol (2004a) offers an excellent overview of the history of online therapy, beginning with the computer program known as ELIZA, which was created by Joseph Weizenbaum at the Massachusetts Institute of Technology in the mid 1960s. ELIZA followed a script that parroted the role of a Rogerian psychotherapist interviewing a new client. While ELIZA is not a true example of computer-mediated communication because the individual actually communicated with a computer and not a real person, ELIZA is the first well documented therapeutic interaction using a computer. Kenneth Mark Colby created PARRY, which simulated a client in therapy who exhibited paranoid behavior. PARRY, differing from ELIZA, could track the flow of conversation. The importance of ELIZA and PARRY is that both demonstrated the first attempts at text-based therapy between computers and individuals. The 1970s and 1980s saw the introduction of bulletin boards, newsgroups and special interest forums, which led to mailing lists (the first listservs) and email as we know it today. Bulletin boards, special interest forums and listservs, as well as the advent of interactive text games, allowing for role-play during the game and socializing with fellow gamers after the game, was also the beginning of people forming virtual communities and groups.

The actual beginnings of advice-giving online by mental health professionals can be traced back to university settings. In 1986, Steve Worona, Assistant Dean of Students at Cornell University developed Dear Uncle Ezra (named after Cornell's founder, Ezra Cornell) and offered computer portals on campus that allowed students to ask questions and receive answers. The questions were answered by university personnel and posted on a bulletin board system for others to read. Dear Uncle Ezra was eventually transferred to the Web and is still in existence today (Uncle Ezra, 2009). Grohol began providing information via Usenet groups in the early 1990s and created the first online index of online mental health support groups. Grohol created Psych Central in the mid 1990s, offering information and self-help. Others began to understand the possibilities the Internet could provide and individuals as well as organizations provided services to assist people in need. In 1994 the Samaritans, a UK-based charity supporting people with suicidal feelings, began offering email services. To this point, mental health advice and services were mostly offered free-of-charge.

In the mid 1990s there emerged a smattering of mental health practitioners who charged for their services; not one single practitioner is noted to be the first, however names such as Leonard Holmes, David Sommers and Ed Needham are noted as part of the initial wave. Richard Sansbury, a psychologist, began offering online therapy services in 1997 and his site is still in existence today (Sansbury, 2009). By 1998, Martha Ainsworth had compiled an online directory of nearly 200 online therapists (Ainsworth, 2002) at metanoia.org, a site created by Ainsworth to offer information to mental health consumers and basic guidelines for practitioners who were developing online therapy websites. The website no longer hosts a directory of online therapists but continues to offer information to consumers and mental health practitioners.

At around the same time private practitioners began extending their suite of services to the Internet, and e-clinics began appearing, offering platforms for therapists and clients to meet and conduct email and chat sessions. The platforms also offered ancillary services such as appointment scheduling, billing and record keeping. Of the six most noted e-clinics at the time, three remain while other e-clinics are moving into the marketplace. LifeHelper.com, etherapy.com, and Here2Listen.com were large e-clinic start-ups that closed during the dot.com bubble period of 1995–2001 in which many dot.com companies were under-capitalized for the long haul. E-clinics of the time spent exorbitant amounts of money on start-up and salaries, including very expensive platforms to host online therapy services. The remaining three, HelpHorizons.com, MyTherapyNet.com and OnlineClinics.com continue to offer a platform for therapists who desire to offer online therapy at the time of writing.

If one searches for varying terms such as online therapy, online counseling, online counselling, online therapist, online counselor, or online counsellor, literally thousands and thousands of websites are revealed. This chapter will discuss how a therapist can begin offering online therapy and offer first steps at setting up services online.

THE IMPORTANCE OF A WEBSITE

Even if a therapist opts to set up a profile on an e-clinic or after reading thus far, has decided not to deliver therapy online, a website is an essential marketing tool for any therapist. Truffo (2007) offers 17 tips for a private practitioner to grow a practice and creating a website comes in at number six. Reviews of other pertinent tips by Truffo are examined further along in the chapter. Bruce (2009a) states four primary reasons a therapist should have a website: educating and informing clients; gathering data; e-commerce; and as a marketing tool. A website may have only one of these functions or encompass all of them at the same time. Education and information is usually combined with marketing strategies to attract clients to the website. Since up to 80 percent of all people use the Internet now to find goods and services (Bruce, 2009b), offering informative and educational information can be a marketing plus. A website is an online brochure with more room than a phone book or newspaper advertisement to state what the client wants to know. For therapists, gathering data usually means offering a newsletter or email updates to visitors in exchange for an email address. Many therapists utilize this feature, often referred to as 'opt-in'. Finally, websites provide an opportunity for merchant portals. For therapists, this means clients can pay for services online prior to face-to-face or online sessions. Truffo (2007) states that 80 percent of a website's content should speak to the client's needs while 20 percent of the content should be about the therapist. She offers a list of six characteristics that top therapist websites share:

1. The therapist speaks about his or her services in a way the client can appreciate.
2. The website offers something for 'free'.
3. The website has a clear 'call to action' and contacting the therapist is easy.
4. The website reflects personality and offers a picture of the therapist.
5. The majority of the content (at least 80 percent) is geared towards the therapist's ideal client.
6. The website is simple and to the point and the therapist is presented in a caring manner.

Whether a therapist is offering consultation or psychotherapy delivered face-to-face or via technology, these six pointers are important for any practitioner's website. Additional tips are available from many resources and among the authors' favorites is Peter Hannah's Free Stuff at www.yourgoogleguy.com offering everything from seven lessons on smart website building to a list of free places to list/link one's website (Hannah, 2009).

Building a website

Once a therapist has decided to have a website, the next step is to determine whether to have the website built or self-build. One factor in deciding is to know that keeping the website current with fresh content that attracts new clients is vital so that the website remains ranked well on search engines. Many people do not update website content because of the Webmaster's charges so being able to make small changes and additions to the website is important (Bruce, 2009b). Whether the website is built by a professional Webmaster or the therapist, the website should allow for easy update to content so that the therapist maintains control of content and can make changes at any time. If the therapist decided to pay to have a website built, many builds can include access to make text changes, add media, etc. While therapists may decide to give the content to a Webmaster or third party to insert into the site, it is key to at least maintain the capability to make additions and changes.

Many website companies in existence offer site editors to customers who want to build a site from scratch or with pre-set templates. The sites www.web.com and www.homestead.com offer hundreds of templates and add-on services as well. When comparing costs of 'do-it-yourself' websites, points to consider include the professional look of sample sites that are offered, how many features the site editor offers and the ability to remove the website editor's branding. Many sites will give a page of links or thumbnails to review in order to gain an idea of the overall style and flexibility of various templates. Comparing features to set-up and monthly fees is important. At the time of writing, a basic website that is self-built can be achieved for less than $30 or £20 per month. Finally, the branding needed on the website is the therapist's branding, not the web designer site's brand. Seeing 'Built by Homestead' or 'This site was built with GoDaddy' takes focus away from the therapist's content and does not offer a polished, professional image to the website visitor. In addition, the domain name should reflect the therapist, not a third party hosting site, e.g. www.janecounselor. homestead.com or www.freewebs.com/~user. If a therapist uses a third party site that displays a particular branding for legitimate reasons, the therapist should still have a website with a domain name that reflects the therapist's practice.

Now that the importance of a website has been discussed, we will talk about e-clinics versus private practice.

DECIDING WHETHER TO JOIN AN E-CLINIC OR PRACTICE PRIVATELY

Once a therapist has decided to conduct therapy online, the next step is usually deciding how the therapist will deliver services on the Internet. Once the basic website is established, how will the therapy be delivered? When a client visits the site, how will the client know how to access the online therapy services? Frankly, many therapists who first start out providing online therapy determine that building a website, marketing a practice and learning about the theory, skills and ethics of online therapy is enough. Any more information added to the already overwhelmed 'therapist as business owner' can be daunting. This is one reason to consider joining an e-clinic. By joining an e-clinic, many of the logistics such as encryption, payment for services, appointment setting and record keeping are handled. Legitimate e-clinics offer encrypted services ranging from email (or messaging) to chat, video and VoIP. Payment is handled by the e-clinic with a certain fee or percentage deducted. The fee is not considered a referral fee, or what some professionals refer to as 'fee-splitting', because the fee the e-clinic retains whether through percentage or a flat fee is being charged to the therapist for use of the platform. Using a pay phone is not free; the customer is charged to communicate. Using an e-clinic's platform is similar in concept. Many e-clinics offer appointment setting options so that the therapist indicates available times and the client can choose and book an appointment. In addition, e-clinics may offer record storage so that transcripts and exchanges are stored on the e-clinic's server, as well as intake questionnaires, progress notes and treatment plans. Some e-clinics offer a billing system to bill clients who use insurance.

Another reason to list on an e-clinic instead of offering services independently is the added bonus of marketing. Derrig-Palumbo (2005) states that a therapist may choose to join an online clinic or may choose to develop a more personalized system and refers to the latter as analogous to setting up a 'brick and mortar' practice. Since many therapists do not start out with enough capital to buy land, engage in heavy marketing and the like, a therapist will often choose to rent a space or join an existing practice with other therapists. With that said, it is the expectation that e-clinics with large numbers of therapists are spending money on marketing their services to potential clients and other therapists. If a therapist decides to list with an e-clinic, once the therapist's profile is created on the e-clinic website, the therapist can then provide the e-clinic link on his or her own website.

An example of the wording on a therapist's site may be:

> I offer online therapy via email and chat. Please click my profile at www.e-clinic.com. Registering as a client on e-clinic.com is easy. You will be able to fill out initial information, book an appointment and pay for a session. As soon as you have booked I will be alerted.

By listing on the e-clinic site and cross-linking on the therapist's own website, search engines will find the therapist's services twice. The therapist may choose to use the e-clinic profile as their primary web address, but again, as mentioned previously, this is advertising the branding of the e-clinic instead of creating an independent presence on the Internet.

Some therapists opt for a profile on multiple e-clinic sites. The reason is likely to be the hope that the more e-clinics a therapist is listed on, the larger the client pool. As well as enhancing the therapist's marketing efforts and visibility on search engines, multiple e-clinic listings may indeed increase potential client referrals. If, however, the therapist is not offering services independently on his or her website, determining which e-clinic profile to list on the therapist's main identifying site may be difficult.

So what should a therapist look for when shopping for an e-clinic to do business with?

1. **Professional Image**: The site should offer a professional image. Generally, therapists and mental health practitioners with credentials and/or training do not want to be lumped together with other self-described 'advice-givers' such as psychics, mystics and other people who give opinions for a fee. While many people may benefit from said advice-givers, mental health practitioners should stand apart from the crowd as health care professionals.
2. **Practitioner Screening**: The site should have a mechanism in place for screening mental health professionals who apply to be listed. Most e-clinics ask for verification of education, certification and/or license along with malpractice insurance information if applicable. By taking these steps, the e-clinic is offering a certain amount of reassurance to the potential client who may sign up for services.
3. **Client Screening**: The e-clinic should ask a basic set of questions to the client upon registration that offers the therapist information related to identity, alternative methods of contact, and suicidality/homicidality. Various e-clinics offer 'instant'

sessions but identity and self-harm/harm to others screening questions should still apply otherwise therapists should opt-out of providing immediate services. Therapists should not list with e-clinics that allow for anonymity unless the e-clinic is actually acting as a crisis hotline and triage. That being the case, the clinic holds part of the liability for client identity and contact in case of an emergency and the terms and responsibilities should be clearly laid out.

4. **Reputation**: Check out the reputation of the e-clinic. Contact other therapists listed on the site. Ask how satisfied they have been with the listing and if they have received any inquiries that led to clients. An e-clinic may have 500 therapists listed but is anyone actually receiving clients?

5. **Solvency**: How long has the e-clinic been in existence? In as much as one can, check the solvency of the company. Are other therapists who utilize the site receiving timely payments after seeing clients?

6. **Marketing**: Is the e-clinic investing money into marketing? Ask the e-clinic for specifics about their marketing plan. Google the name of the e-clinic and the entire website address.

7. **Reliability**: Ask about the reliability of the service. Have other therapists experienced frequent technology breakdowns? When visiting the site, do all links open and are all menu tabs on the site functional? If the site were to go down, what measures would the e-clinic administration take to alert therapists and clients who might not otherwise have a mechanism to contact each other.

8. **Record Storage**: Ask the e-clinic what measures are taken to ensure confidentiality of records beyond the encrypted measures taken for the purpose of therapeutic exchanges. Is the server that stores information owned by the company? If not, where is the server located?

These eight points offer a therapist a way to perform a simple audit of any e-clinic. Keep in mind, most e-clinics are probably not used to being asked these questions but over time experience has shown that these are key points that should be considered if opting for an e-clinic listing.

Finally, when using the services of an e-clinic, the therapist should consider backing up client records and exchanges and maintaining client intake and identification information separately from the e-clinic site. Check the Informed Consent, terms of use, privacy statement and other information offered by the site to ensure that the policies and procedures of the e-clinic coincide with ethical and legal responsibilities.

PRIVATE PRACTICE – OFFERING A MORE PERSONALIZED APPROACH

Therapists may choose to offer a more personalized service that clients can access through the therapist's website. This can be accomplished relatively easily now with low-cost and free encryption services. Unless a therapist has unlimited funds, the need to create a tailored platform for therapeutic exchanges is not necessary. However, even the cost of building such platforms has significantly reduced since the late 1990s and early 2000s. Many therapists simply want to offer online therapy to existing clients who may from time to time benefit from the convenience of chat or email. Other therapists may want to create a sub-practice within their existing face-to-face practice to expand their ability to serve a wider pool of clients and to diversify revenue streams. Still other therapists desire to deliver services exclusively online. Whether providing adjunct services to existing clients, creating a sub-practice or practicing exclusively online, a more personalized service is possible. For an example of online therapy as a sub-practice, see one of the authors' websites at www.deeannamerznagel.com – all of the basic components discussed below are incorporated into the site and may be reviewed by therapists who are contemplating offering a more personalized approach.

Begin with the basics.

1. **Therapeutic Exchanges**: How will therapeutic exchanges take place? A number of free and inexpensive options exist. For a full list of options, simply Google 'encrypted email' or 'encrypted chat' as examples. But for the purposes of this chapter a few options will be discussed. Hushmail (www.hushmail.com) offers free and fee-based services and is as easy to set up as a gmail or yahoo email account. Both the client and the therapist must have Hushmail accounts for the exchange between the two parties to be encrypted. Hushmail also offers encrypted chat. Skype (www.skype.com) is another free service offering encrypted chat, video and VoIP. Cryptoheaven (www.cryptoheaven.com) is yet another service that for a fee, offers encrypted email and chat. The best way to determine ease of use it to set up an account with various services and try them out. If possible, exchange an email or engage in a chat with a friend or a colleague. Some programs offer much richer applications than others. For instance, Hushmail's chat program does not offer emoticons or change of text color options, while Skype is rich with chat options but does not offer email or message capabilities.

2. **Appointment Setting**: Decide how to schedule appointments. For therapists with existing face-to-face practices, will the same business hours apply for online clients? Will face-to-face and online clients be able to set appointments online? Does the therapist prefer an email requesting a certain time or even a phone call? Work out the logistics of appointment setting and then consider calendar programs such as genbook (www.genbook.com).

3. **Payment Methods**: Determine how you will receive payment. It is advised that payment always be received before the service is rendered. Many merchant options exist for online purchasing and two of the most popular and user friendly are Google Checkout (http://checkout.google.com/sell) and Paypal (www.paypal.com). Neither of these services requires the merchant to set up a merchant account through a bank and the fees per transaction are reasonable. If a therapist already has a merchant account or otherwise takes credit card payments from face-to-face clients, that service may be adaptable for use on a website. Whatever method is utilized, make sure the credit card information is captured in a secure and encrypted manner. Be sure to specify fees for service on the website and if offering a lower fee for online therapy than for face-to-face therapy, offer an explanation. Otherwise, there may be the misunderstanding that online services are not as valid as face-to-face services. Offering an explanation such as lower overheads, no lost travel time, no incurred travel costs, etc. may prove to be helpful.

4. **Client Screening and Forms**: Determine how the client will be screened. An Intake Questionnaire can either be built into the site or created through a

form-building service such as www.getenhanced.com that can host the completed form on a secure site. Another option is to advise the client to set up an encrypted email account and once the client has set the email up, a questionnaire can be emailed. Whatever the option, the information should be sent via encrypted channels. Other forms such as Informed Consent and Privacy Practice statements should be available to the client on the website. Ideally, a web page is created for the Informed Consent (sometimes referred to as Terms of Use, Terms and Conditions or Terms of Agreement) and also a downloadable version is made available for the client. A check box that indicates receipt and understanding of the Informed Consent can be included on the aforementioned questionnaire. If the therapist requires an original signed copy, initial receipt can be acknowledged on the online questionnaire and a signed copy can be faxed or mailed. The Informed Consent should include statements discussed in the previous chapter. One of the authors' Informed Consent form is available at www.deeannamerznagel.com as a downloadable word document and as a web page entitled Terms and Conditions. While this consent is offered courtesy of that author, seeking legal consultancy prior to implementing all or part of the document is strongly advised to ensure it relates to the service being planned.

Once these basics are in order, the therapist can begin to build the content of the website. When building the content, think in terms of giving concrete, explicit and easy to understand instructions. Imagine a potential client visiting the site. How will the client know where to go on the site and what to do next? In addition to reviewing the author's website cited above, visit other online therapist websites. Review sites for content, ease of understanding and use, and overall appeal. Use the ethical framework in the previous chapter to ensure the website includes all necessary components and then begin to incorporate the content that covers the basics discussed here.

BEYOND THE WEBSITE: ADDITIONAL MARKETING STRATEGIES

The website is built. Services are in place. How will potential clients make their way to the virtual office door? Therapists who offer online therapy should embrace the Internet as the primary way to advertise services and specialties. After all, potential online clients are not likely to respond to a locally placed advertisement in a newspaper or magazine.

Beyond the six characteristics of a top therapist websites (see above, p. 75), Truffo (2007) offers 'Seventeen things you can do to grow your practice'. While some of the ideas she offers relate more to a face-to-face practice, several on her list apply to online therapy practices. The list below incorporates Truffo's applicable ideas and a few others.

1. **Online Therapist Directories**: Referred to as the new Yellow Pages, directories offer search engine placement and in most cases, a website listing. Some directories are free; others charge a yearly or monthly fee, while others are a benefit of membership. Those mentioned here are just a sampling just represent the directories that would be most beneficial to online therapists. It is advisable to be listed in as many directories as possible, provided the cost is not prohibitive.

a. Psychology Today (www.psychologytoday.com) offers a Therapist Directory and the therapist can create a short biography and describe their services. This directory is one of the largest in the United States and offers an encrypted forum to therapists who have a directory listing. Most of the therapists listed offer primarily face-to-face services. Psychology Today's directory generally ranks high in the search engines.

b. Find-a-Therapist.com (www.find-a-therapist.com) also offers a Therapist Directory. In a similar way to Psychology Today's directory, the therapist can create a profile page and potential clients can search the database. The directory offers international listings.

c. The National Directory of Online Counselors (www.etherapyweb.com) offers listings of online practitioners within the United States as well as a listing of each state licensing board. The site is small but proactive, offering resources and information to consumers and professionals alike.

d. ACTO (www.acto-uk.org) offers a Therapist Directory that is searchable by special interest (categories of client issues such as relationships or anxiety) or alphabetically. Therapists list qualifications in both offline and online training (verified by the association), and also information about experience in working online. The focus at the ACTO directory is online therapy costs only, although most members work in other arenas.

e. Online Therapy Institute's Web Directory (www.onlinetherapydirectory.net) offers listings of member therapist websites and e-clinics that follow the Online Therapy Institute's Ethical Framework. The directory has hundreds of listings in over 30 categories, and offers a free listing for not-for-profit organizations. The directory is not limited to online therapy websites, it also offers listings of training organizations, online supervisors and consultants, for example.

2. **Blog**: A blog is like a website but the content is updated frequently and search engines love blogs. Use a blog to post about specific topics and encourage people to comment. Think of the blog as a constantly evolving brochure that is placed at various new places every week. Every time a blog is updated and lands in a blog directory, on Google or in Google's blog directory, someone else finds it. Be sure to link the main website to the blog.

3. **Pay-Per-Click Advertising**: Some therapists have found this method of paid advertising to be effective but keywords for online therapy can be quite pricey so be sure to read more information about how to market with Pay-Per-Click effectively.

4. **Use Audio**: More and more business and service websites are offering audio options to welcome new visitors. A pleasant voice can be attractive to some potential clients. Make sure the audio feature is a choice and not an automatic plug-in.

5. **Ask Questions**: Ask questions on the home page that reflect the interests and needs of a potential client. This can be a good marketing strategy and the search engines will pick up on the key words in the questions. Other potential clients will be led straight to the site if they Google a question or similarly phrased search.

6. **Offer Free Information**: Some therapists offer tip sheets, such as '5 Key Ways to Beat the Winter Blues' or '10 Stress-busters'. Use an opt-in email request form to capture the visitor's email address and begin building an email list for newsletters and special events. Popular campaign programs include Constant Contact (www.constantcontact.com) and Campaigner (www.campaigner.com). Other free services might include a free 15–30 minute initial consultation via phone or chat.

7.   **Become a Local Celebrity**: If you are the only therapist in your area offering online therapy, consider soliciting local newspapers and magazines to write an article about your services. Include the benefits of online therapy in the interview.

8.   **Write Articles**: Write articles that reflect a specialty area and submit to key online article databases such as Ezine Articles (www.ezinearticles.com). This will boost search engine results. Even consider distributing articles locally, tapping into the local celebrity idea. Local clients may be intrigued by the idea of having a therapist nearby that they can see online but still close enough for a face-to-face appointment if necessary.

9.   **Create a Podcast**: A podcast is like an online radio show that is created much like an audio recording would be created. The podcast can be uploaded to podcasting services like itunes.

10.   **Consider a Press Release**: Write a press release that talks about specialism with the writing of the press release geared toward the ideal client. Discuss the ways services are delivered, whether face-to-face or online. Use a press release distribution company that gives strong results such as Mass Media Distribution (www.mmd newswire.com).

11.   **Join Social Networks**: Join in on social networking sites. Social networking is a great way to socialize with friends and colleagues. The more people who know what services are available, the more potential for referrals. Be careful of boundaries on social networking sites. While some sites are suited for friends and colleagues, the same sites may not be suitable for marketing to clients. Keep in mind that some social networking sites for professionals are closed so that only other professionals on the social network can see your profile, while other social networking sites are open, allowing for the network to function as both a social network and a directory. Whatever the case, keep profiles professional and follow the ethical framework from the previous chapter with regard to accepting invitations from clients or potential clients. See below a list of social network sites to consider joining:

   a.   Facebook (www.facebook.com). Therapists using this site should monitor permission and security levels so that clients and potential clients cannot access therapist information.

   b.   Twitter (www.twitter.com). This is a great micro-blogging site that offers opportunities for peer and professional development.

   c.   LinksforShrinks (www.linksforshrinks.com). A networking hub for therapists, counselors, life coaches, and healing arts practitioners to build and market their private practice online.

   d.   MedXCentral (www.medxcentral.com). A medical industry social network, networking the medical and health care online universe and providing professional and social networking in health care.

   e.   Therapist Leadership Institute Online Community (www.tliconnect.com). A site which aims to improve the lives, careers and reputations of therapists worldwide.

   f.   Therapy Networking (www.therapynetworking.com). Online networking for therapists.

   g.   Online Therapy Institute Social Network (www.onlinetherapyinstitute.ning. com). A site for the Online Therapy Institute's members and friends interested in bringing together technology and mental health.

12. **Create a Presence in Second Life**: While this may seem far off the beaten path, a small build in Second Life can serve as another extension of a website; essentially a three-dimensional way to advertise services. Services do not have to be facilitated in Second Life to have a presence that will increase exposure to traditional online therapy services. Many health-related businesses and organizations are setting up shop in Second Life offering education and information (Nagel, 2008). Certainly, security issues should be considered if services are offered in Second Life or any virtual world that exceed more than a consult and move into a therapeutic exchange, but for advertising purposes, Second Life can be fun and cutting edge. Potential clients are already Internet confident.

Finally, another key point to add to the marketing conversation is that of suggesting ongoing professional development as part of the marketing strategy. By connecting with other colleagues and peers, each of whom has individualized specialties and skill sets, a sense of expertise is born. Becoming a seasoned online therapist helps marketing pursuits. Take these steps (Nagel, 2007) to become an expert:

- Obtain formal training about online therapy.
- Consider a certification or other marker that demonstrates proficiency.
- Consider ongoing clinical supervision specific to online therapy.
- Engage in peer supervision.
- Participate in research projects.
- Join organizations that offer peer support and disseminate new information about the field.
- Contribute to the field by adding to the existing body of literature, educate others and advocate global empirically based research and therefore understanding of the modality.

Other issues related to the business of online therapy are much like the issues related to the business of therapy. Legal and ethical consult are advised when necessary. Solid business practice is warranted and patience in building one's practice is needed. Therapists should keep up with emerging trends in the field and keep abreast of new business trends such as drawing up a 'professional will' (Psychotherapy Finances, 2007). Choose an executor of client records so that estate assets are protected in the event of death.

After nearly a dozen years of online therapy being offered on the Internet, the wave has only now begun. Therapists seeking to 'cash in' should take heed, and while his cautionary note does seem rather negative, Grohol (2004b) makes valid points. To many, online therapy is a new experience, which still entails lingering difficulties and concerns, both legally and ethically. Grohol states that those of us who choose to offer therapy online are 'virtual pioneers'. He cautions that online therapy is still an emerging field, and the point to be taken is this: be serious and devoted to online therapy as a viable and useful modality to clients. Supplementing an income or working from home should not be one's first motivation for doing this work. After all, as Truffo (2009) points out in a recent article about the therapy practice of the future, independent practitioners may need to look beyond the billable hour and begin to incorporate multiple streams of revenue, developing new ways to help our clientele, through products such as e-books, CDs, and e-courses that enhance services we may already provide on or offline. Our motivation should be guided by our intrinsic desire to serve people and our community while leveraging our time and energy.

We have now offered the theory, skills, ethics and business strategies for being an online practitioner. In the next chapter, we shall offer a single case study which aims to highlight some of the issues inherent in online practice while illustrating how it can be experienced, using various communication methods, in a flexible but professionally contracted way.

REFERENCES

Ainsworth, M. (2002) 'E-therapy: History and Survey', in *ABCs of 'Internet Therapy'*. Available at www.metanoia.org/imhs/history.htm [accessed 8 April 2009].

Bruce, M. (2009a) 'How a Website can Serve your Business', in *Websites for Counselors*. Available at www.counselorwebsites.com/SmartCorp/webflexor/articles/generic/How%20a%20Website%20can%20Serve%20Your%20Business.pdf [accessed 8 April 2009].

Bruce, M. (2009b) 'Being your own Webmaster', in *Websites for Counselors*. Available at www.counselorwebsites.com/SmartCorp/webflexor/articles/generic/Being%20Your%20Own%20Webmaster.pdf [accessed 8 April 2009].

Derrig-Palumbo, K. (2005) 'Online Therapy: the Marriage of Technology and a Healing Art', in S.M. Harris, D.C. Ivey and R.A. Bean (eds), *A Practice That Works: Strategies to Complement Your Stand Alone Therapy Practice*. New York, NY: Routledge.

Grohol, J. (2004a) 'Online Counseling: a Historical Perspective', in R. Kraus, J. Zack and G. Stricker (eds), *Online Counseling: A Handbook for Mental Health Professionals*. San Diego, CA: Elsevier Academic Press.

Grohol, J. (2004b) *The Insider's Guide to Mental Health Resources Online*. New York: Guilford Press.

Hannah, P. (2009) 'Free Stuff', in *Your Google Guy*. Available at www.yourgoogleguy.com/free stuff.htm [accessed 8 April 2009].

Nagel, D.M. (2007) 'Who can Perform Distance Counseling?', in J.F. Malone, R.M. Miller and G.R. Walz (eds), *Distance Counseling: Expanding the Counselor's Reach and Impact*. Ann Arbor, MI: Counseling Outfitters.

Nagel, D.M. (2008) 'Health Education and Intervention in a Virtual World', in *Telehealth World*, 1(3): 8.

Psychotherapy Finances (2007) 'The Value of Having a "Professional Will"', in *Psychotherapy Finances*. Available at www.psyfin.com/articles/1207livingwill.htm [accessed 8 April 2009].

Sansbury, R. (2009) 'Headworks', in *Headworks*. Available from www.headworks.com [accessed 8 April 2009].

Truffo C. (2007) *Be a Wealthy Therapist: Finally You Can Make a Living While Making a Difference*. Saint Peters, MO: MP Press.

Truffo, C. (2009) 'Pink-Spoon Marketing: A Model for the Therapy Practice of the Future', in *Psychotherapy Networker*, 33(2): 42–29.

Uncle Ezra (2009) 'Dear Uncle Ezra', in *Cornell University*. Available at ezra.cornell.edu/posting.php [accessed 8 April 2009].

6
CASE STUDY

INTRODUCTION

The following is a case study that is a fictional composite for illustration purposes. The authors of the text role-played this scenario, one as therapist and one as client. It should be noted that the authors express caution about the use of role-play and case simulation when teaching and demonstrating online therapy in Chapter 7. The authors, fully aware of the disinhibition effect and having been working partners for several years, felt comfortable each taking on a role with the other, and used well-known debriefing tools after each session. Still, when demonstrating this intense level of work, emotional safety must always be considered regardless of the working relationship and professionalism of the role-players.

The theoretical orientation of both authors is psychodynamic and this is evident throughout the dialogue. The authors offer a short case due to limits of this project and to also define how a psychodynamic approach can be incorporated into short-term exchanges. While this client may ultimately benefit from longer-term therapy online or off, it becomes clear that she benefited from the few exchanges offered and that the therapist was able to provide closure even within the short timeframe.

The authors have incorporated a web link to a book that could translate to bibliotherapy with more ongoing sessions. Issues related to confidentiality and technology breakdowns are highlighted within the case study. To capture both asynchronous and synchronous text-based therapy, this scenario includes both chat and email exchanges. As the text is taken verbatim from the sessions, the vagaries of writing — such as typos — have been included to illustrate clearly what such work can be like.

CASE STUDY

Mary is 55, is married, and has two children — a son of 19 who is at university and a daughter aged 14. She manages the Payroll Department of a local supermarket full time in North Manchester. Her history includes being raped by a stranger as a teenager, which she has never disclosed. This has caused ongoing problems of intimacy in her relationships and depression, for which her medical doctor prescribes anti-depressant medication. Mary's feelings of not coping have escalated recently and her relationship with her husband, although loving, is suffering, as she feels unable to discuss anything to do with her increasingly difficult feelings with him. She is also very nervous of discussing her issues with a stranger face-to-face, as she feels that would be unbearably intimate and she is uncomfortable leaving the house apart from for the purpose of her occupation.

Mary Googles the symptoms of severe depression and ways of seeking help for it on the Internet. She discovers that online therapy is available and decides this could be ideal for her, as she assumes that having a therapeutic relationship from her work computer would keep the issues from her husband and daughter on their shared home PC.

Having visited a few websites that offer email and chat room sessions with individual practitioners, she decides upon a female therapist in the USA, as the distance makes her feel safe, the free downloadable software recommended is encrypted and she can pay online securely with her credit card. Mary peruses many websites and chooses Clara Lang, not just because of the geographical distance but also because she is able to verify Clara's credentials, read about how online therapy works, and download forms straight from Clara's website. She completes a detailed online application form, held on a secure authenticated server, which includes not only personal details but also emergency contact details and her medical and psychological history (Figure 6.1).

At the bottom of the form, Mary clicks the checkbox to say that she has read the Terms & Conditions and also the Privacy Practice Statement. After she clicks SUBMIT she receives an automated response.

THANK YOU for your Online Submission to

Clara Lang, Therapy Online

Be sure to schedule your appointment for voice, chat or in-person sessions.

If you have chosen email therapy, I look forward to receiving your first email exchange through HushMail.

I will respond to your first email exchange within 2 business days.

Intake Form
Today's Date: 2/12/2009

CLIENT INFORMATION		
Last Name	First Name	Middle Initial
Flynn	**Mary**	**B**
Nickname	Marital Status	Passport or other ID#
Mary	**Married**	**123568**
Birth Date	Age	Gender
05/09/1954	**55**	**Female**
Drivers License State/#	Occupation	Employer
n/a	**Payroll Manager**	**Supermarket**
Street Address		P.O. Box
56 Acacia Street		
City	State/Country	Postal Code
Manchester	**UK**	**M1 2AB**
Home Phone #	Other Phone #	Email Address
01234 567890	**07780 123456**	**maryflynn@aol.com**
Can we leave a message on your home phone?		**No**
Can we leave a message on other phone?		**Yes**

REQUESTED SERVICE INFORMATION	
What service(s) is requested at this time? Counseling:	**Individual**
Are you interested in traditional face-to-face counseling, distance therapy or a combination of both? Face-to-face counseling depends on your location and my availability.	**Distance**
What concern has prompted you to contact me at this time?	
I'm not coping with things. My depression seems to be worse but I can usually cope with it ok. It's affecting my relationship with my husband, I can't talk to him.	
If you are requesting distance services, why are you interested in distance counseling rather than traditional face-to-face counseling at this point?	
My husband doesnt know about this and he will if I see someone nearby – he works from home nd knows my routine with work. I don't go out apart from work. I have a work computer i could use? My daughter also uses this PC as welll as him. I don't want to see someone, it's too hard to talk	

(Continued)

FIGURE 6.1 (Continued)

Please check all that you have experience with:
Email, Instant Messaging / Chat , Encrypted email or chat, Payment for items/services online.
What type of platform does your computer use?
Windows XP,
What type of internet access do you have?
Broadband (cable, DSL, satellite)

IN CASE OF EMERGENCY		
Who should be contacted in case of emergency?		**Beth**
Relationship to patient	Home Phone #	Work Phone #
Friend	**01234 567000**	**01234 098765**

INTAKE/BACKGROUND INFORMATION	
Have you ever been in treatment with a therapist or counselor in the past?	**Yes**
If so, when were you treated and for what problem(s)?	
My doctor referred me two years ago cos i was depressed and after six months i got an appointment but it was too hard to talk so i stopped going	
What was the result of this treatment?	
I stopped going	
Are you being treated by a therapist, counselor, or psychiatrist now?	**No**
Are you experiencing any negative feelings or 'symptoms' at this time, e.g. feeling anxious, depressed, sad, angry, frustrated, etc?	**Yes**
How severe would you say your symptoms are?	**Severe**
What have you already tried for this problem?	
nothing apart from seeing my doctor	
Have you tried anything that DOES help?	**Yes**
If 'Yes', what DID help?	
My friend Beth helps a lot and takes me to Bingo which i love	
Are you currently taking any psychotropic medication (e.g., anti-depressants or anti-anxiety medication)?	**Yes**
If so, what type of doctor prescribed it?	**Physician**
Have you taken any psychotropic medication in the past?	**Yes**

Please list all medications you are now taking, including the dosage. Please include prescriptions, over-the-counter, herbal, homeopathic medications and nutritional supplements.	
I have prozac from my doctor and i take vitamins daily to encourage my daughter to do the same. The prozac package says 20mg? I have an inhaler for asthma attacks	
How often do you drink alcoholic beverages?	**Frequently**
How often do you use recreational drugs?	**Never**
Please list below all recreational drugs you use.	
We have wine with our meals in the evening? Is that frequent? I smoke about 15 cigarettes a day	
Have you ever been hospitalized for drug or alcohol abuse, a suicide attempt, 'nerves' or other mental health Concern?	**No**
If 'Yes', please give dates and circumstances:	
If you are married or have a 'significant other' or long-term partner, how long have you been together?	**24 years**
Please describe your relationship:	
I love my husband and he loves me. We have a happy if quiet life and rarely row. He is very supportive of me and how i feel but i can't talk to him about it and that makes him sad which i hate	

If you have any children, please list their names and ages:			
Name:	**Mark**	Age:	**19**
Name:	**Jenny**	Age:	**14**
Name:		Age:	
Name:		Age:	

Who lives in the household with you?:			
Name:	**Geoff**	Relationship:	**Husband**
Name:	**Jenny**	Relationship:	**Daughter**
Name:		Relationship:	
Name:		Relationship:	

Do you have any brothers or sisters?	**Yes**
If so, where are you in the sibling order?	**Youngest**
Where do your siblings live and how do you get along with them?	
My sister lives in Preston about 45 minutes away. We get on ok but i dont see her much. We talk on the phone probably at least once a fortnight	
Are your parents alive?	**Yes**

(Continued)

FIGURE 6.1   (Continued)

How do you get along with them?	
Fine, they live nearby and I visit twice a week	
Do you have in-laws?	**Yes**
How do you get along with them?	
Fine, my mother-in-law is dead but my father in law is alive but lives in Scotland with his second wife so we only see him on family occasions really	
How much education have you completed?	**Some College**
If you are a student now, please complete the following 2 questions:	
Which school do you attend, how are your grades and how do you like school?	
If you are in college or graduate school, what is your major?	
Are you happy with your current job/career?	**Yes**
If not, why?	
What jobs/careers have you done in the past and how did you like them?	
I've work at the Supermarket for over 10 years, i started when Jenny started school. I didn't work before that except helping Geoff out with administrative stuff for the warehouse he runs	
How many times have you moved in the past year?	**None**
How is your overall health?	**Good**
If you have any medical problems now or in the past that would be helpful for me to know about, please describe:	
I don't think so, just some mild asthma which i use an inhaler for	
Have you ever been arrested or convicted of a crime?	**No**
If 'Yes', please explain:	
It would be helpful to know about your family of origin, what your childhood was like, and anything else about what your family and life were like when you were growing up. (If your past history includes abuse of any type, please include this.)	
My childhood was fine until i was 14, then I couldn't talk to anyone anymore and became very introverted and stopped taking care of myself, wearing black, hiding etc, and my mother didn't know what happened which made her angry at me all the time. I was attacked at that point near to school in Preston. I nearly told my sister but she had stuff going on cos she is older than me by five years so she was going to Uni etc. I married early to leave home and because i found someone who seemed to love me and i loved him and it made my mum happy cos she didnt want to deal with me anymore. My dad ignored the whole thing so it was easy for me not to have to tell anyone what happened, just put up with my mum being annoyed and angry with me until i left home	

Were you ever physically or sexually abused as a child?	**No**
If so, by whom?	
I don't know the answer to this, I was attacked but not abused?	
Are you being physically or sexually abused now?	**No**
If so, by whom?	
Have you ever felt in the past like harming yourself or somebody else?	**No**
Do you have those feelings now?	**No**
Is there anything else about you that I should know?	
I have a habit of tearing at my nails and hair but I'm not sure if that is harming myself?	

AGREEMENT
I have read and completed this form truthfully and accurately as to the best of my knowledge. I have read the Terms and Conditions and Privacy Statement.
I have read and agree with the above disclaimer.

FIGURE 6.1   INTAKE FORM

Clara, having received the questionnaire, has time to review Mary's responses before receiving the first exchange. She also takes time to set up the client file. She uses an encrypted flash drive which holds pertinent documents and information such as the initial questionnaire and chat transcripts. She also takes time to perform an Internet search for emergency and referral services in Mary's locale. Since the client and the therapist live in different geographical locations, Clara ensures she has emergency phone information at the ready. She also performs a cursory search of therapists in Mary's geographical area should a face-to-face referral be appropriate. This information is saved to the client's file and Clara also bookmarks any relevant websites for future reference. In creating this file ahead of time, Clara is demonstrating due diligence in providing the best standard of care.

Mary composes her email from her work computer the following day.

From: maryflynn@hushmail.com

To: Clara@hushmail.com

Date: Sat, 14 Feb 2009 18:01:28 + 0000

(Continued)

(Continued)

This message is encrypted, and is digitally signed by 'maryflynn@hushmail. com' <maryflynn@hushmail.com>.

Hello,

This is my new email address with Hushmail as per your instructions. I would like to communicate via email rather than chat and have paid through Google Checkout.

I guess you know my details from the form, so I'll just say a little bit more. I just don't feel like I'm coping and I don't have anyone to talk to about it. My best friend Beth is great but we just go out really, Bingo occasionally and that sort of thing. My doc gave me Prozac a while back and I saw a counsellor a couple of times. But things seems to have got worse for me recently. I cant talk to my husbanc, Geoff, which makes him really sad and that also makes me unhappy. I think I need to talk about the attack I mentioned when I was 14, I've never told anyone about it and I think that is a mistake now. I couldn't tell the other counsellor, I just couldn't find the words aned I didn't feel safe.

My eldest boy is at university and seems to be settled well. My daughter Jenny is lovely but I worry about her a lot and all the time. Actually I never stop worrying about her at the mo. She's only 14 and she thinks she 35!! I want to keep her safe, but she spends time in chatrooms etc and I don't know that she is.

I think that's all for now I need to get back to work.

Thanks,

Mary

Clara responds to Mary within the 2-business-day window, welcoming Mary to the process and briefly reviewing informed consent, attaching the Informed Consent document again for emphasis. Rather than reviewing in detail through the first email, Clara opts to summarize key points that can be found within the document. During the exchanges, Clara points to informed consent issues along the way as necessary. In this exchange, Clara advises Mary against using her work computer due to issues related to confidentiality.

From: Clara@hushmail.com

To: maryflynn@hushmail.com

Date: Mon, 16 Feb 2009 14:10:31 +0000

This message is encrypted, and is digitally signed by 'clara@hushmail. com' <clara@hushmail.com>.

Hi Mary,

Welcome to Therapy Online. I am so glad you have decided to reach out at this time. You are taking a brave step for yourself and I realize how big this step is for you. If you have not done so already, please be sure to read the Informed Consent which is attached as a word doc for your convenience. Most of the information is basic but the document does tell you more about how I work, issues related to your confidential therapy record, and how to handle an emergency.

Mary, you stated that you share a computer at home but you do not want your family to know you have sought counseling. You referred to a computer at work that you might use which may offer privacy from family and convenience for you but I should caution you that using a work computer is not the best choice. Even if you use an encrypted web-based email service, your employer may have taken other security measures such as a keystroke tracking device.

Would it be possible for you to use your home computer and let your family know you are spending time researching a hobby or subject? The other option may be to tell your husband since it appears from your statement, 'He is very supportive of me and how i feel but I can't talk to him about it and that makes him sad…' that he might understand. Letting him know that while you are not ready to talk about your feelings, but that you are reaching out might relieve his concerns a bit.

I am glad you have sought out your doctor for an anti-depressant. I am thinking that maybe you could talk to your doctor about your increased feelings of depression and as you describe, 'I have a habit of tearing at my nails and hair ...' and no, that is not necessarily intentional self-harm. If this behavior is troubling to you I can forward additional information. Just let me know. In the meantime though, if your inability to talk with your husband and your depression is affecting your relationship with your husband your doctor might be able to increase your dosage of current medication

(Continued)

(Continued)

or try another medication that might be more effective while we continue our work here. Would you be willing to do that?

Mary, I did note that you referred to an attack that occurred years ago. Did you receive counseling or any support at the time? Do you think this incident has affected you emotionally? Do you feel the attack ties into your fears or feelings of depression, or worry about your daughter now? If you do, I want you to feel safe talking with me here about that because your email contained feelings of being unsafe for both you and your daughter.

I look forward to hearing your response.

Take good care,

Clara

From: maryflynn@hushmail.com

To: Clara@hushmail.com

Date: Thur, 19 Feb 2009 15:53:29 +0000

This message is encrypted, and is digitally signed by 'maryflynn@hushmail.com' <maryflynn@hushmail.com>.

Hello Clara,

Thank you for writing to me, it means a lot to hear you think I am being brave. I admit I've been nervous in thinking abt what you would say, and funnily enough was thinking about the work computer thing before you said about it. When i sat down to email you a response, someone came into my office even tho the door was shut and they know not to disturb me in that case. It gave me a bit of a jolt to be yanked back into work. So I was thinking of how I could use the home one secretly.

Then I got your email and thought about the keystroke tracking thing (I googled it) and although I could ask my boss about it (we get on really well), I then thought that doing this secretly at home would be just that – another secret. And if *I* have secret computer use, how can I expect Jenny to be honest about her use?! So i made a big dinner for the three of us and we talked abt using computers safely, which was good. I made a deal with them that we would tell eachother abt any use of the PC that we thought others should know about, and <<with a deep breath!>> I said that I had been very down recently and so I was talking with someone qualified but objective over the Internet, and I hoped it would make me feel better. Geoff didn't seem very surprised, actually, and he said 'fine if that will help you feel better' and that was great – I nearly cried <<v. nearlly crying now remembering it>>. So we all know I'm here with you at times and they know i want to be alone to talk to you.

i don't want to increase my medication unless this doesnt help me. I think it will tho – I feel quite comfy talking to you like this, as Jenny and I chat a lot and I'm used to how it works. Anyway, what the dinner conv brought up was talking about talking to strangers online – she uses the teen version of SL or something similar i cant remember offhand, and I cant say I approve of how she looks there. I realised I was getting a bit upset and then remembered your email, and it occurred to me that I am really bad with strangers, whether they are talking to me OR to her. And her online life is full of strangers isn't it? Maybe thats why I worry about her so much all the time, people aren't always what they seem to be, I should know.

Jenny will be 15 soon and it occurred to me that I have been feeling this bad since she turned into a 'full fledged' teenager at 14. Does that sound strange? Maybe thats just coincidence. But its true and as I was attacked at her age i do take yr point that *that* could be why I'm feel like this and it *is* tied in. No, there was no support at that time, I didn't tell anyone. I kept it to myself and just started covering myself up in dark baggy clothes and spending a lot of time in my room. My sister went to University and so I lost my big sis, who i ideolised <sp? soz>. I just dont know how to tell you what happened, it seems stupid to affedct me now when it was so long ago – 40 years!

I've spent a lot of years just thinking of it in terms of 'the attack' or 'when that happened'. i think i get scared of opening the floodgates, becuawse if i do and its bad i'm no use to jen in keeping her safe from strangers who are out to hurt her badly. The man at the school gates back in Preston seemed nice enough, but he hurt me badly. Do you get what i mean i don't want to write the word. I do feel safe here but it's such an ugly word.

I'll answer your other questiosn becuase I'm feeling a bit shaky now. The hair and nail thing doesn't really bother me that much – i just do it more when I get stressed out (have done since the attack now I think about it). But it's not an issue except my husban nags me about it lol.

looking forward to hearing from you,

Mary

Clara's next response to Mary begins to prepare Mary for dealing with past trauma. Safety and containment are offered as Clara begins to pace the work and set the tone for regulating Mary's emotions as needed.

From: clara@hushmail.com

To: maryflynn@hushmail.com

Date: Mon, 23 Feb 2009 12:38:54 +0100

This message is encrypted, and is digitally signed by 'clara@hushmail. com' <clara@hushmail.com>.

Dear Mary,

I hope this email finds you well and of strong spirit. As I read your last email I was struck with how open and honest you are being – with your family, with me and with yourself. You are talking from your heart and I sense a great desire on your part to know yourself better. That is such a great step because when you know yourself you are able to be genuinely present in all of your relationships!

The family dinner was a great way to tell those you care about the most what you are up to and to bring topics to the table (secrecy, computer use) that can be dicey for teenagers. But you brought the topic up as it related to you and what a great witness to your daughter! I hear what you are saying about her 'other' life in a virtual world. It is different than when we were coming up isn't it? But this virtual living has become such a part of our social fabric now. The relationships she creates online are no less 'real' than her face-to-face relationships, really. Years ago, we had pen pals. Here is what I suggest. Have a talk with your daughter about safety online; about boundaries and the idea that anything placed online carries forever – that it never goes away. Ask her to just consider this before she says or posts anything on a website or in a virtual world. Her avatar – the persona she portrays online – that is her way of expressing a part of herself and so I would monitor that judi-ciously. If she is dressing provocatively, consider this normal for her age. Talk with her over lunch or a shopping trip about who she is online – engage her in a way that will invite her to communicate with you and keep talking! Because open communication is the key.

Mary, it is very possible that you are feeling the way you are right now because your daughter's age is a trigger for you – bringing you back to an earlier time in your life that was unpleasant. In some ways you may be re-living that experience emotionally over and over and it may feel like you are re-living those feelings. But you have great insight and you recognize this. Again, talking about it safely will help take the power away that the event still has over you. Does that make sense? You do not need to dis-close details to me or anyone. But talk about how you feel, the word(s) you dare to say. Once you name it and put it out there, then it is yours to put in a box and place on a shelf, throw in the trash or burn – anything you want to do metaphorically to rid your life of the bad thing. It doesn't mean the memory is gone, or that the scar does not remain, but the act – the event, the trauma, the attack will have far less power over you. And in that way you will be able to be fully present for your daughter and offer the insight and protection she needs.

Now, as you read this, and when you write again, you might feel shaky or disoriented as you described at the end of your last email. Know that you are ok and that you are safe. When you start to feel disoriented, pull out your nurturing side (the side that takes care of your family in a loving and gentle way) and turn that nurturing to yourself.

Warmly,

Clara

From: maryflynn@hushmail.com

To: clara@hushmail.com

Date: Fri, 27 Feb 2009 18:58:55 +0100

This message is encrypted, and is digitally signed by 'maryflynn@hush-mail.com' <maryflynn@hushmail.com>.

Hi Clara,

Thanks for your response. I do feel open and honest since the meal! And I've been thinking about what you said about me wanting to know myself better. I do want that, you know … I feel like I've been in a bubble all these years, life just going on because it has to and the world didn't stop just because of the attack – it was me who stopped :o(

You've been very reassuring about the stuff with Jen and the virtual stuff. I don't know how she would take to telling me about her online life (I mean what it means to her – I feel secure about the fact we can keep it in the open). I think I kind of feel that everyone needs their privacy at that age and although I need her to be safe, I don't want to pry. BUT having said that I do take on board the issues around whatever she says being around forever on these sites and think it good to remind her of that.

(Continued)

(Continued)

But hten that applies to this as well doesn't it? What I say to you will be around for ever, including talking about the attack? I like my honesty, but it will still be around and although I feel that I could do that safely with you, I'm not sure that having tghat stuff around would be good if the family came across it (I know this is all secure, but I am TERRIBLE at leaving stuff lying around lol!)

I was wondering if having a chat scheduled would work? I do want to talk about the attack with you, I'm just nervous of doing so here (I mena in an email). I like the idea of renaming it and then the power being different – I hadn't thought of it like that. And I thought that maybe doing that with some-one who is like there at the same time, that would work better for me – only to get past that point, mind. I like talking like this. But if someone is there at the actual time I can say it – that would be better?

I'm off work next week after Monday and will be around a lot. Could we do it then?

Thanks,

Mare

At this point in the process, Clara considers Mary's request and invites her to engage in encrypted chat for a 50-minute session the following week, for which Mary pays a one-off fee. Clara offers instructions on how to set up the chat session and maintains a genuine and caring tone.

From: clara@hushmail.com

To: maryflynn@hushmail.com

Date: Mon, 2 Mar 2009 12:38:54 +0100

This message is encrypted, and is digitally signed by 'clara@hushmail.com' <clara@hushmail.com>.

Hi Mary,

I think scheduling a chat at this point is an excellent idea. I use Skype for chat because it is easy to use and is encrypted. If you do not have an account, you can create one at www.skype.com. You can schedule a chat time using my online appointment book. My Skype username is *ClaraLang*. I look forward to talking with you in real time!

Best,

Clara

However, at the appointed time, Mary does not appear in the chat room, despite an email to her from Clara reminding her and restating instructions to attend the session.

Remembering that Mary's intake form states that Clara may contact her via mobile phone but not the landline, she considers telephoning her as she is slightly concerned for Mary's emotional safety in light of the content of the previous email session and Mary's wish to discuss the attack. However, as the relationship has thus far taken place via text only, she is hesitant to call because sometimes interjecting voice into a relationship that has been strictly text-based can interrupt the therapeutic alliance.

Since the use of texting was covered within the Informed Consent as appropriate for housekeeping correspondence, Clara decides to text Mary via SMS with a simple neutral message, that also underlines boundaries with regard to the use of text messaging, that reads:

Sorry we missed each other. Let's reschedule. Text or email back with good time.

By using the return receipt feature on her mobile phone, Clara knows that Mary has received the text even if she has not yet read it. She receives a text back promptly that states:

Soz, Jen downloaded koobface virus from FB – PC being seen 2. Same time 2mrrw ok with u? M

Relieved that the missed session was down to a technical issue, Clara texts back to confirm that the following day would be available for her. At the appointed time, Mary arrives at the chat room a few minutes early for her session via encrypted Skype Chat where Clara is waiting for her.

During the chat session, Clara offers the opportunity for Mary to disclose her story in a safe and contained way, yet prepares Mary for the possible feelings of vulnerability that may follow the disclosure. This chat represents a 50-minute session. When working with trauma issues online, additional minutes taken to the full hour may prove helpful in assisting the client with containment before closure.

[12:30:00 PM] Clara says: **Hi Mary**

[12:30:16 PM] Mary Flynn says: **Hi Clara – thanks for agreeing to meet up again**
[12:30:25 PM] Mary Flynn says: **really sorry abt yesterday**

[12:30:50 PM] Clara says: **That is fine – it happens with technology! I am glad we were able to reschedule for today**.

[12:31:14 PM] Mary Flynn says: **good – i think I said Jen downloaded the virus from facebook?**
[12:31:23 PM] Mary Flynn says: **THAT was a learning curve for us all**

[12:31:40 PM] Clara says: **Yes – I hope you have resolved that issue. And with that, the technology glitch and your concern about the security of email, I just want to assure you that because we use encrypted email, your communications are as secure as when you purchase something at a website and use a credit card.**
[12:31:45 PM] Clara says: **Does that make sense?**
[12:31:55 PM] Clara says: **I also hear that you think chatting might be easier for some issues.**

[12:32:09 PM] Mary Flynn says: **yes, thanks – perfect sense I'm learning a lot doing this!**
[12:32:31 PM] Mary Flynn says: **I think that I've really understood yr points abt owning stuff**
[12:32:47 PM] Mary Flynn says: **and so being able to control it**

[12:32:56 PM] Clara says: **very good–**
[12:33:12 PM] Clara says: **How do you think communication is going with your daughter?**

[12:33:37 PM] Mary Flynn says: **i think we're fine – with the virus happening in particular we had another chance to talk about safety**
[12:33:39 PM] Mary Flynn says: **online i mena**
[12:33:41 PM] Mary Flynn says: **mean**
[12:34:20 PM] Mary Flynn says: **i think she thinks I'm a little overcautious but then i was able to say to her more abotu safety and stuff overall**

[12:36:43 PM] Clara says: **well if you can communicate about her online life in a way that appears that you are interested instead of a prying mom, that will be helpful.**

[12:36:50 PM] Mary Flynn says: **yeah that seems to work**

[12:37:01 PM] Clara says: **She will give you some information and she will decide what mom does not need to know.**
[12:37:26 PM] Clara says: **But it is also a way to indicate to her that you 1. care and 2. pay attention**

[12:37:32 PM] Mary Flynn says: **i still worry abt her**
[12:37:53 PM] Mary Flynn says: **but i think we reached a point where she can keep herself safe**

[12:37:54 PM] Clara says: **I know – but you are doing what you need to do.**

[12:38:06 PM] Mary Flynn says: **or as safe as possible anyway**
[12:38:15 PM] Mary Flynn says: **we text a lot these days so i know where she it**
[12:38:17 PM] Mary Flynn says: **is**

[12:38:22 PM] Clara says: **You are laying a foundation for her and teaching her responsibility.**

[12:38:40 PM] Mary Flynn says: **yeah – maybe i should have had someone do that for me**

[12:38:53 PM] Clara says: **So Mary, you said you wanted to chat because you thought it might be easier to tell me about your assault.**
[12:39:03 PM] Clara says: **(now you are doing it for yourself!)**

[12:39:09 PM] Mary Flynn says: **:O)**
[12:39:20 PM] Mary Flynn says: **bit scary**
[12:39:27 PM] Mary Flynn says: **but built meself up for it today**

[12:39:34 PM] Clara says: **What can we do here to make it safe for you to talk about it?**

[12:39:39 PM] Mary Flynn says: **and the others know to leave me alone for the next hour**
[12:39:47 PM] Mary Flynn says: **it's nice to talk to you live!**

[12:39:49 PM] Clara says: **good so you are in a quiet place**

[12:39:52 PM] Mary Flynn says: **yeah**

[12:40:30 PM] Clara says: **Mary- do not feel compelled to tell details. My concern is that details can retraumatize you.**
[12:40:50 PM] Clara says: **So tell me generally what happened, be aware of your feelings while you tell and know that I am here**

[12:40:57 PM] Mary Flynn says: **i dont think i could be retraumatised... i feel like i've been traumatised for ever**

[12:41:02 PM] Clara says: **you can chunk the information in short bits if that helps**

[12:41:05 PM] Mary Flynn says: **but i want to get rid of that now**
[12:41:10 PM] Mary Flynn says: **no I'm ok**

[12:41:12 PM] Clara says: **ok**

(Continued)

(Continued)

[12:41:35 PM] Mary Flynn says: **tehre was this bloke who used to hang around the school**
[12:41:42 PM] Mary Flynn says: **we all talked to him**
[12:41:52 PM] Mary Flynn says: **seems odd now but in those days it was different**

[12:42:12 PM] Clara says: **yes**

[12:42:16 PM] Mary Flynn says: **but everyone talked to him - bioys and girls and even the teachers sometimes**
[12:42:28 PM] Mary Flynn says: **i think we all thought he was fine cos everyone talked to him**
[12:42:36 PM] Mary Flynn says: **can u imagine that happening now?**
[12:42:53 PM] Mary Flynn says: **Jen pracitcally has to show her passport to get into classs lol**

[12:43:16 PM] Clara says: **It is good we have better boundaries around schools now for sure!**

[12:43:22 PM] Mary Flynn says: **yes - that's reassuring**
[12:43:55 PM] Mary Flynn says: **so i'd been chatting to him over a while and he just was walking with me away from the school**
[12:44:16 PM] Mary Flynn says: **my friends (didnt have that many) walked a different way home**
[12:44:24 PM] Mary Flynn says: **and i was glad of the company now i think abt it**
[12:45:00 PM] Mary Flynn says: **and we sort of tookt he shortcut past some woods**
[12:45:10 PM] Mary Flynn says: **well not really woods - more of a pond and copse**

[12:45:11 PM] Clara says: **ok.**

[12:45:29 PM] Mary Flynn says: **and he just suddenly grabbed me**

[12:45:49 PM] Clara says: **that must have been startling!**

[12:45:59 PM] Mary Flynn says: **i didnt know what was going on**
[12:46:10 PM] Mary Flynn says: **one min we were talking - no idea about what**
[12:46:22 PM] Mary Flynn says: **the next we were within the trees and i was on the ground**
[12:46:56 PM] Mary Flynn says: **now i think of it, i think being so suddenly startled was the most confusing thing**

[12:47:11 PM] Clara says: **do you remember what you felt like when you found yourself on the ground?**

[12:47:34 PM] Mary Flynn says: **confused and i banged my knee quite hard**
[12:47:39 PM] Mary Flynn says: **so that hurt**
[12:47:53 PM] Mary Flynn says: **i remember thinking someone had fallen on me**

[12:47:54 PM] Clara says: **yes I can imagine both the confusion and the pain.**

[12:48:22 PM] Mary Flynn says: **from the tree (that actually happened to my big sister once at the same place – lad in a tree fell out and hit her, hurt her back)**
[12:48:54 PM] Mary Flynn says: **so i thought that was what was going on that the hand over my face was to stop me crying out in pain**
[12:49:01 PM] Mary Flynn says: **god i was niave**

[12:49:27 PM] Clara says: **Fourteen year olds should be allowed their naivety**

[12:49:40 PM] Mary Flynn says: **yeah but it seems so obvious now**

[12:49:57 PM] Clara says: **Of course because you are peering in on the experience with adult eyes**

[12:50:02 PM] Mary Flynn says: **i think i said in one of my emails that think the worse and that was what it was**
[12:50:16 PM] Mary Flynn says: **i see it now.**
[12:50:23 PM] Mary Flynn says: **god this is hard**

[12:50:37 PM] Clara says: **Mary – let's take a break for a moment.**

[12:50:41 PM] Mary Flynn says: **ok**

[12:50:42 PM] Clara says: **Breathe.**

[12:50:44 PM] Mary Flynn says: **that would be good**

[12:51:02 PM] Clara says: **I am sensing that you feel overwhelmed so will you let me pace this experience for you**
[12:51:07 PM] Clara says: **?**

[12:51:09 PM] Mary Flynn says: **I'm going to get a glass of water i've drunk this one is that ok?**

[12:51:18 PM] Clara says: **Indeed**

[12:51:20 PM] Mary Flynn says: **brb**
[12:52:50 PM] Mary Flynn says: **k, I'm back thanks**
[12:51:53 PM] Mary Flynn says: **you can pace this better?**

(Continued)

(Continued)

[12:52:44 PM] Clara says: **well I think for this session you have given me enough of the story. And what I would like to do now is talk a bit about the feelings behind the story so far.**

[12:52:48 PM] Mary Flynn says: **ok**

[12:53:13 PM] Clara says: **Then I want to make sure you are feeling good about self before we end the session.**

[12:53:18 PM] Mary Flynn says: **ok thats fine**

[12:54:15 PM] Clara says: **So, what you have described is this: someone you trusted (doesn't matter what you know NOW as an adult – the 14 year old little girl trusted this person) caused you harm and instilled great fear in you,**
[12:54:43 PM] Clara says: **Without me knowing anymore of the story, I know that in that moment you were terrified.**

[12:54:51 PM] Mary Flynn says: **yes**

[12:55:11 PM] Clara says: **And there were more moments to come. So the experience was a series of terrifying moments**

[12:55:16 PM] Mary Flynn says: **yes**

[12:55:22 PM] Clara says: **Can I ask you a question?**

[12:55:25 PM] Mary Flynn says: **yes**

[12:56:03 PM] Clara says: **Do you feel anxious much? Or, maybe not really anxious in the purest sense of the word, but do you well, startle easily?**

[12:56:53 PM] Mary Flynn says: **i feel anxious all the time but worse than that i think that the person i was before wouldnt be**
[12:56:57 PM] Mary Flynn says: **does that make sensse?**
[12:57:04 PM] Mary Flynn says: **he changed me**

[12:58:07 PM] Clara says: **Yes. Here's how it makes sense to me. That experience became imprinted on you- not just your memory of the event- but it became imprinted at a soul-level. Some would even say a cellular level,.**
[12:58:19 PM] Mary Flynn says: **ok...**

[12:58:38 PM] Clara says: **It is like the fear gets trapped. And part of you grows up into the reasonable and responsible adult that you are–**
[12:58:55 PM] Clara says: **but that frightened 14 year old got trapped**
[12:59:10 PM] Clara says: **and was never able to truly escape the experience**

[12:59:20 PM] Clara says: **Now it is time to release her from that fear.**

[12:59:31 PM] Mary Flynn says: **yes i see what yr saying**

[12:59:40 PM] Clara says: **It is somewhat symbolic but also very real.**

[12:59:47 PM] Mary Flynn says: **how can i do that?**

[12:59:58 PM] Clara says: **It takes practice...:)**

[1:00:03 PM] Clara says: **But–**

[1:00:08 PM] Mary Flynn says: **:) thot it might**

[1:00:08 PM] Clara says: **here is how to start.**

[1:00:13 PM] Mary Flynn says: **ok**

[1:00:30 PM] Clara says: **Be aware the next time you feel scared, fearful or anxious.**
[1:00:52 PM] Clara says: **Let the adult part of you do that 'check' – sort of like you did when you said 'Seems so obvious now...'**
[1:00:57 PM] Clara says: **remember earlier in the chat?**

[1:01:01 PM] Mary Flynn says: **yes!**
[1:01:02 PM] Mary Flynn says: **oic!**

[1:01:15 PM] Clara says: **Look into your feelings with that rational adult part of you.**
[1:01:52 PM] Clara says: **If you look in and see that it is the 14 year old inside who is scared then nurture that part of you just like you would your daughter**
[1:02:19 PM] Clara says: **The first step is being able to recognize the feeling that is attached to the event**

[1:02:24 PM] Mary Flynn says: **ok**

[1:02:53 PM] Clara says: **Then next is being able to be the parent to yourself – the nurturing adult to yourself – who was not there to protect you then in that moment**
[1:03:05 PM] Clara says: **It is a way of 'reframing' the experience**

[1:03:10 PM] Mary Flynn says: **yes – wehn i found out Jen was talkign to a stranger online i was more thatn startled, i was like a deer in headlights**

[1:03:46 PM] Clara says: **ok. And part of that fear is reasonable. We have fear to alert us! But part of that fear comes from your own experience**

[1:03:50 PM] Mary Flynn says: **so like i do with Jen except i need to do it in reverse?**

(Continued)

(Continued)

[1:03:58 PM] Mary Flynn says: **no not reverse – like retrospct?**

[1:04:09 PM] Clara says: **It is a bit of self-talk.**

[1:04:12 PM] Mary Flynn says: **yes i see**

[1:04:24 PM] Clara says: **That can be literal or you can talk to yourself quietly.**

[1:04:44 PM] Mary Flynn says: **sometimes i say 'come on Mare, get it together already'**
[1:04:55 PM] Mary Flynn says: **but i could be nicer than that to me i spose**

[1:04:57 PM] Clara says: **But if you can imagine the little girl inside you – scared in that moment – then also imagine what you as a nurturing parent would do in response.**

[1:05:04 PM] Mary Flynn says: **yes!**

[1:05:18 PM] Clara says: **Instead say, 'Mary, you will be ok because I am here and will keep you safe.'**

[1:05:38 PM] Mary Flynn says: **i like that a lot**

[1:06:02 PM] Clara says: **Good. I am glad that feels like a fit for you.**

[1:06:16 PM] Mary Flynn says: **yeah – cos i do that with Jenny so I can do it for me as well**

[1:06:28 PM] Clara says: **That is right!**

[1:06:30 PM] Mary Flynn says: **and if i can keep her safe i can certainly keep me safe**
[1:06:40 PM] Mary Flynn says: **i just always thought to keep her safe which is fine**
[1:06:48 PM] Mary Flynn says: **but i can keep me safe as well**

[1:07:11 PM] Clara says: **And in keeping yourself safe you will have more to give to her.**
[1:07:41 PM] Clara says: **So we have covered alot of ground today. I want to make sure you are ok.**

[1:08:08 PM] Mary Flynn says: **i feel excited actually – its nice to think of it positively rather than this (that?!) big black cloud**

[1:08:41 PM] Clara says: **Sometimes when we disclose feelings about things we have never or rarely talked about it causes us to feel vulnerable.**

[1:09:00 PM] Mary Flynn says: **i feel ok – i think cos i didnt have to talk abt the detail**

[1:09:05 PM] Clara says: **So if in the next day or two you feel 'exposed' – like you told a secret or like it was unsafe to tell, that is normal.**

[1:09:07 PM] Mary Flynn says: **thanks for that i thot i would have to**

[1:09:27 PM] Clara says: **Mary, do you like to read?**

[1:09:32 PM] Mary Flynn says: **i have a lot to think about**
[1:09:38 PM] Mary Flynn says: **yes i do when i get the time**

[1:10:52 PM] Clara says: **Ok- I am going to make a book recommendation. Let me know how you like it. But I do caution not to read this sort of material late at night before bed.**

[1:11:00 PM] Mary Flynn says: **oh ok**
[1:11:06 PM] Mary Flynn says: **sounds like a horror movie lol**

[1:11:14 PM] Clara says: **When you read, do this when you are fresh and then take time like we did here to get centered**

[1:11:21 PM] Mary Flynn says: **ok**

[1:11:30 PM] Clara says: **No actually it is good nurturing reading but it can have a tendency to drudge up feelings.**
[1:11:41 PM] Clara says: **And I don't want your sleep to be interrupted.**

[1:11:50 PM] Mary Flynn says: **ok – the family are getting used to giving me time when i need it now**

[1:11:59 PM] Clara says: **The feelings are good – but when they come up it can be ...startling sometimes.**

[1:12:07 PM] Mary Flynn says: **so i have a kinda space after dinner to do this sort of stuff**

[1:12:12 PM] Clara says: **So take time for yourself like we have talked about here.**

[1:12:28 PM] Mary Flynn says: **I'll be prepared for the startling**
[1:12:53 PM] Mary Flynn says: **what is the book?**

[1:13:23 PM] Clara says: **Here is the link to the book:** http://www.amazon.com/Inner-Bonding-Becoming-Loving-Adult/dp/0062507109/ref=sr_1_7?ie=UTF8&s=books&qid=1238519413&sr=1-7
[1:13:31 PM] Clara says: **it is called Inner Bonding.**

[1:13:34 PM] Mary Flynn says: **ok**

[1:13:52 PM] Clara says: **Becoming a Loving Parent to Your Inner Child.**

(Continued)

(Continued)

[1:14:04 PM] Mary Flynn says: **oh thats rather nice!**

[1:14:06 PM] Clara says: **Captures much of what we talked about today.**

[1:14:07 PM] Mary Flynn says: **nice title**
[1:14:14 PM] Mary Flynn says: **yes i can see how it would**
[1:14:26 PM] Mary Flynn says: **thanks ! :)**

[1:14:29 PM] Clara says: **So, are you feeling centered?**

[1:14:47 PM] Mary Flynn says: **yes i feel fine i think – Geoff is cooking dinner and Jen's doing homework**
[1:14:57 PM] Mary Flynn says: **they have a pact to clear up so i can have a bath'**
[1:15:14 PM] Mary Flynn says: **i feel like part of the family more these days**
[1:15:27 PM] Mary Flynn says: **rather than the person who 'they don't get'**

[1:15:28 PM] Clara says: **Ok good! -**

[1:15:38 PM] Mary Flynn says: **yes its very good**

[1:15:52 PM] Clara says: **Would you like our next exchange to be email or chat?**

[1:16:13 PM] Mary Flynn says: **i think i'd like to think about it and send you an email when I've thought about all this?**
[1:16:17 PM] Mary Flynn says: **is that ok?**

[1:16:59 PM] Clara says: **Absolutely! And by the same token, I may suggest we take up a particular issue in chat. Would that be ok with you?**

[1:17:16 PM] Mary Flynn says: **yeah sure**

[1:17:32 PM] Clara says: **I have a better sense of how you process with email and chat now. And I think the combination could be beneficial.**

[1:17:47 PM] Mary Flynn says: **ok**

[1:17:48 PM] Clara says: **Ok so I will wait to hear from you in an email.**

[1:18:03 PM] Mary Flynn says: **good – I'll have a look at the book as well**.

[1:18:11 PM] Clara says: **It is a pleasure working with you! Take care and have a great dinner!**

[1:18:23 PM] Mary Flynn says: **Thank you so much I'll be in touch**

[1:18:24 PM] Mary Flynn says: **bye**

[1:18:29 PM] Clara says: **bye**

Following the chat session, Mary takes some time to think through what was discussed and follows up by ordering the book Clara suggested, having looked at the previews available at Amazon (www.amazon.com). She decides that having been able to talk about the attack with Clara in session without needing to be explicit about the details, she now feels able to sit quietly with her husband and share with him some of what happened to her as a child. The talk goes well and they decide to explore further options in face-to-face couple counseling to enable them to communicate better with regard to intimate problems, and to find a way that Geoff can help Mary with coming to terms with her past and the reasons for her depression and anxiety. Mary sends a final email to Clara.

From: maryflynn@hushmail.com

To: clara@hushmail.com

Date: Wed, 04 Mar 2009 10:27:34 +0100

This message is encrypted, and is digitally signed by 'maryflynn@hushmail.com' <maryflynn@hushmail.com>.

Hi Clara,

Firstly can I say thanks so much for the chat session we had, it has really made a difference. I did feel a bit disorientated for a bit, but I think I know why – I felt that the time had come to be done with this – well, its never going to be done cos it happened but to be done with dealing with it in this way. I've ordered the book you suggested and read some of it at Amazon, it looks really interesting. And I'm really grateful that I was able to talk about the attack without all the details of it, so I thought well if I can do that with Clara maybe I can do it with Geoff!

So we sat down after jen had gone to bed, with a bottle of wine, and we had a really long talk about everything – the depression, the medication, and I was able to say something about what happened to me all those years ago.

(Continued)

(Continued)

Again, no details and he said he didn't need details but felt that it was difficult to understand what happened without them. So I said to imagine the worse and he could understand that. He was lovely – so supportive and angry on my behalf but also sad for me. We also talked about the sessions you and I had and he said that since that dinner when I told him I was talking to you he had done his own research on the internet about counselling and therapy and said he had a better understanding of it.

He has suggested that in order for him to help me as much as possible in dealing with all this that we try to get an appointment for couple counselling somewhere around here in the UK. What do you think? I don't know how that wouold work online although I see that some therapists do offer it, but then I also think it would be good for us to do something together that we can follow up with treating ourselves (looking after our inner selves!!) afterwards like a meal or something.

I've found a local agency and we made an initial appointment. So I think that this has been brilliant but I would like to try that next rather than book further emails here. Thanks again for all your help, its made a big change and I think I can build on that and maybe come back to you if I need to?

Thanks, Clara!

Mare

Clara offers a final exchange with encouraging words and an invitation to return in the future for further therapy online. Clara also includes a satisfaction survey link should Mary opt to give anonymous feedback on her online therapy experience.

From: Clara@hushmail.com

To: maryflynn@hushmail.com

Date: Fri, 06 Mar 2009 11:59:51 +0100

This message is encrypted, and is digitally signed by 'clara@hushmail.com' <clara@hushmail.com>.

Dear Mary,

I am so glad you have found this experience helpful! You seem much more centered now and it is good to know that you are communicating so openly with your husband!

I think it is great that the two of you are seeking couples counseling and I see how you could follow up each session with dedicated time between the two of you. Online couples counseling works a couple of ways – either through chat but instead of 2 people, there are 3 people engaged in the conversation – or through email exchanges like this. With email, the partners each write to the therapist and the therapist responds openly to both in one return exchange. If you decide at any time that you want to try online couples counseling, I can offer a referral for you.

You are absolutely welcome to revisit anything we have discussed in the future. As you continue to nurture yourself, other feelings and concerns may emerge. This is normal. You have carried your feelings for a long time and it may take awhile for you to feel an internal sense of order so to speak. So please don't hesitate to contact me again.

Mary, I wish you all the best!

Clara

If you would like to fill out a satisfaction survey, please <u>click here</u>. Your name and other identifying information is not required. The survey is anonymous. I strive to provide quality services and these questions help me understand how services may be improved.

This concludes the case study. As with any therapeutic case, many directions could have been pursued but the key is demonstrating authenticity through whatever modality or technique is employed. Therapists who work online can bring their perspective and skill set to this work as demonstrated through Clara and Mary. While it is not within the scope of this book to delineate every possible angle, one can imagine that within this case study alone, Clara may feel the need to seek out clinical supervision or one-off case consultation. Mary may decide to continue her work with a face-to-face therapist. Perhaps couples therapy will prove to be beneficial and sufficient to bring closure to Mary's experience of her traumatic assault. One might postulate that in years ahead, Mary might be triggered again by a life event or a perceived emotional threat and may contact Clara to begin work again. This case study was developed to give a face to theoretical discussions about what truly does transpire during synchronous and asynchronous text-based therapy.

Continuing on to Chapter 7, one will be reminded early on about cautions regarding role-play when training and demonstrating online therapy. The next chapter reviews ways in which a therapist can gain the necessary training and education that will enhance proficiency as an online therapist.

7
TRAINING ONLINE THERAPISTS

INTRODUCTION

In this chapter, we shall consider training to work in this field, from both modalities – online and offline (face-to-face). As training opportunities grow and branch into training for other technologies, whole programs are being developed to meet the need of this rapidly growing part of the profession. It is important for the practitioner to assess what levels of post-graduate training are required to be effective and ethical online, and what their responsibility is in gaining Continuing Professional Development hours (CPD) and/or Professional Continuing Education (CE credits). As Goss and Anthony (2004) state, familiarity with email and chat for business and personal use does not mean a qualification in online therapy.

While training for online counseling is not recognized as part of the core training to be a counselor or psychotherapist, it *is* recommended as post-graduate training. Wilkins (2006) points out that further training is desirable because however good core training was, it is bound to have gaps and become dated, which is certainly true where technology is involved. Nagel (2007) also supports the view that while therapists may have excellent skills and be accustomed to accessing numerous theories within their work, it is wise to seek training to pre-empt the variety of new challenges that are likely to occur. The BACP's 2009 Guidelines strongly recommend that post-qualification training is undertaken, so that practitioners have undertaken some specialist training in online therapy and are competent to work within this specialized area. Such training would normally take place after the therapist's core practitioner training and would be admissible for Accreditation in the UK as Continuing Professional Development.

Tyler and Sabella (2004) make an interesting point about the availability and flexibility of online therapy in that it could pressure the profession – and those who govern it – to formulate international licensure or certification, which would facilitate uniform standards of training. They state 'Cybercounseling may very well become the impetus for the ultimate in counselor credential portability'.

ONLINE TRAINING

The power of online training, regardless of the topic, does not come from the technology alone. The power of learning online is unleashed when trainers and facilitators know how to use technology to create better instruction. There exists an entire pedagogy around the concept of e-learning (Waterhouse, 2005). A learner-centered online approach to training combines blended technologies, both synchronous and asynchronous. Technology is seen as a valuable tool and when the technologies are well blended, the learning experience is enhanced. The use of blended technologies helps to accomplish the following (Lehman and Berg, 2007):

- Better fulfill specific learning objectives
- Create course efficiency
- Provide flexibility
- Appeal to different situations, content, and learning styles.

When offering training online about conducting online therapy, the approach and use of blended technologies with therapy trainees as the audience can help guide the course development. Thinking about one's own classroom experience can be helpful. Literally think about learning within the confines of four walls and then visualize and think about a virtual classroom. Think about the course content being taught in a traditional classroom setting that may or may not offer the ability to use PowerPoint or access the Internet. Then think about taking the same content and applying blended technologies. What enhances the material? Where are asynchronous technologies helpful and when are synchronous technologies most beneficial?

Of course, training for online work is mostly undertaken online, which is sensible since the potential online counselor needs immersion in a world without a physical presence. In a fast-changing field such as online therapy, the resources and training for being a practitioner need constant updating, which is much more possible online than through any materials in print. In addition, the obvious benefit of an online course includes overcoming geographical location, and in many cases – for courses which rely exclusively on asynchronous communication between trainees and with the trainers via email and forums – the time zone differences between countries.

There are also disadvantages to online courses. Technical glitches do happen, hardware may not be sophisticated enough to run the course, trainee or server error means that coursework does not get saved, access dates can get easily missed if not open-ended, and links outwith the course are often changed or get taken down. There is also a possibility of someone other than the trainee actually doing the work if passwords are shared. Some in-house training depends heavily on the philosophy or client base of the organization (or in-house trainer) and is insufficient for a more objective general online therapy service.

Course appearance

Bloom and Waltz (2000) define several features of training online, and point out that 'only imagination and finances limit a developer'. These include, but are not limited to the following.

Webinars

New or existing videos can easily be inserted into a web page for viewing as an adjunct to the course, or as part of a course itself. This may be a lecture or examples of software in action to help the trainee navigate the course. Vlogs (video logs) can also be a useful addition to enhance the trainees' experience, although this does allow an element of physical presence to exist, which may not be preferable to a 'pure' text-based environment. These can also be provided on CD-ROM or DVD if bandwidth is limited.

Live broadcasts

Again taking into account the possible preference of a non-physical environment for training an online therapist, live lectures can be broadcast and a whiteboard used for trainees to post questions or comments. Interactive online conferences are also a good resource for practitioners, with trainee commentaries taking place in chat while the presentation is going on. Live audio broadcasting to a PowerPoint presentation is also very successful, and the presentation can be supplied for download.

Linking

Course materials such as academic papers can be linked to within the course via hyperlinks, or links to other websites as an example of what an online therapy website looks like, allowing critical analysis of service provision as part of a course.

Themes

Visual icons can be very useful to guide a trainee through the course, indicating important or controversial points with a red triangle for example, or a yellow question mark to indicate where coursework needs submitting.

Coursework input

Online text inputting boxes allow all the trainees' work to be kept safely on a server, allowing access for the trainer where necessary. This is particularly useful if the trainer feels that the trainee is struggling with a concept and can step in via other methods, such as email, to give extra support or feedback.

Take-the-test

Online tests are simple to implement, and useful to assess the trainees' learning at the end of a module. The software, with the scores and/or grades being collated and sent to the trainer, can score these automatically, and immediately. These can be scheduled tests or taken at the trainees' convenience. These are often multiple-choice tests, but can also be short answer or essay format. A test bank of questions, where questions are selected randomly, is also often useful. Practice tests can also offer immediate feedback if an answer is wrong and provide the correct answer to aid or correct the learning.

Student tracking

Enrolment on a course, including initial application, money transactions, start and end dates, and password use can all easily be automated. The trainer can have access to logs of when the trainee was online doing the course and how long was spent there, as well as logs of all communications and submitted coursework.

Forums

Trainee forums, with topics such as Networking, Clinical Issues, Technical Issues, Course Issues, etc., are very useful for sharing resources and gaining peer support in a remote environment, particularly if self-motivation starts to flag, as seems to happen more often in an online environment (Bloom and Waltz, 2000). Trainees can often feel deskilled at first in what is often an unfamiliar, even alien, environment.

Forums also provide a good network for practitioners post-training, particularly as a sense of togetherness has been fostered during progress through the course. Many of these contacts are working in different locations across the world and so provide an interesting commentary on international issues. They are also good for trainer-to-trainees communication in broadcasting news or changes to the course without having to email individuals.

Chat rooms

In-course chat rooms are another good way of talking to other trainees and the trainer in synchronous time, either by just going in to see who is there spontaneously or by scheduling a chat via an online calendar system or discussion at the forums.

Bookstores

Constantly updated bookstores and further reading archives are useful for up-to-date resources, and can also provide a small revenue stream if done through a larger company such as Google Checkout or Amazon.

Wikis

Course wikis can often be a useful place for posting information gathered during the course by trainees, with editing and extension by others (including the trainer). The discussion pages behind the published wiki pages can often be used as a committee space in deciding the 'truth' or decided opinion about something relevant to the topic.

Virtual worlds

Courses are now being offered in virtual worlds such as Second Life. Within a virtual world, live broadcasts, streaming videos, PowerPoint presentations or pre-recorded webinars can be offered with the added experience of a virtual physical world. Synchronous interaction can take place among participants and between the facilitator and the participants. Kay (2009) offers the following summary of virtual world training:

> The unique qualities of a 3D virtual worlds [sic] can provide opportunities for rich sensory immersive experiences, authentic contexts and activities for experiential learning, simulation and role-play, modelling of complex scenarios, a platform for data visualisation and opportunities for collaboration and co-creation that can not be easily experienced using other platforms.

Course content

Training courses for transferring therapeutic skills to working online vary, but a pragmatic approach is to choose one that includes theoretical elements of online work, applicable ethical issues, and which has an element of experiential exercises. As Jones and Stokes (2009) point out, there are many 'hidden' issues before beginning online work, and the authors agree that it is not until a trainee is going through a course that they discover what they don't know or what hadn't even occurred to them as possibly being an issue. Consider these statements from trainees at Online Counselors.co.uk (our italics):

> I have benefited enormously from this course. *There were so many aspects that I hadn't even considered* and writing this piece has really helped me do what it says on the tin – bring it all together. Thank you.

My initial thoughts when reflecting on my experience of the course is just how surprised I was by the depth of the information and the breadth of the topics covered ... *Many of these issues would not have occurred to me at all in advance of the course* and I am grateful to be made aware of them and to now have some understanding and training around them.

I never thought I knew how to do internet counselling but I *have become aware of aspects that I simply hadn't considered.*

(www.onlinecounsellors.co.uk/links.html)

The flexibility of online training means that courses can be taken at the trainees' convenience. This is not as applicable for training that relies on synchronous communication between trainees, for example those that take place in a virtual world setting or use role-play. Indeed, there is a certain debate about role-play itself as a suitable training exercise when training online. The arguments for it are that it is usually a part of core training and there is evidence for its importance in therapist training to gain experience in a new career, and further, that when done properly it can be an effective and stimulating way to practice and learn (Keith-Spiegal et al., 2002). Indeed, role-play is routinely used in many areas of training and is, for example, a key assessment tool essential in medical education to ensure practitioners are competent before being unleashed on real patients.

However, the responsibility for self-care by the trainees and trainee care by the trainers should be paramount, with facilities for debriefing or coping with any personal material or issues that have arisen as a result of doing role-plays. Grauerholz and Copenhaver (1994: 140) note 'experiential methods often require a greater degree of personal disclosure than is required in more conventional methods such as essay examination and research papers'. In online training, this is particularly relevant due to the heightened sense of safety because of the perceived distance and therefore the disinhibition effect taking place. Where interviews for core therapy training would usually flag up any unresolved mental health issues that may be triggered by experiential work, online trainings tend not to have that process in place. Blatner (2002) identifies role-playing as a 'technology for intensifying and accelerating learning; it is like electric power tools in relation to carpentry'. As such, it takes an extremely secure and safe environment, with a group who have absolute trust in the trainer and other participants, for role-play to take place successfully online. Balleweg (2000) cites Weiss (1986) as noting that students have difficulty role-playing authentic clients, which limits the quality of the learning experience for the 'therapist'. Lane (2000) suggests the unusual possibility of using actors to role-play clients, which seemed beneficial to both parties, although possibly cost-prohibitive for the online training organization and which would probably need a whole new training course in online acting itself.

Some trainings do not use role-play at all because of the possible harm to trainees in them revealing personal material as part of the process, instead preferring to use actual anonymized client material in the case of email work and simulated real chat room therapy sessions where the trainee is the observer, rather than the therapist or client. Feedback from trainees indicates that this is a successful method of experiential training. Using observational material in training courses means that the 'script', logged from an actual live therapy session, can be interrupted at various points with comments and questions from the trainer which are automated into the software. Trainees can arrange to meet in chat rooms to practice using the environment outside of the course material itself but within the course facilities. This low-level experiential type of chat room training allows trainees to be immersed in the session and learn from expert and experienced online therapists, without the anxiety of 'getting it right' in role-play sessions.

OFFLINE TRAINING

Face-to-face, or offline, training takes place in various ways, from presentations at conferences to full two-day workshops or more. Many professionals are accustomed to attending in-person trainings for professional development. Creating a dynamic face-to-face training course is often a challenge as people who have already faced the responsibilities of home and work are then sometimes forced to attend a training that requires focus, often in an uncomfortable or sterile environment.

Goodman (2006) conducted a survey of workshop participants and after analyzing responses to open and closed-ended questions, he was able to identify five factors as the most problematic for presentations. He called these problems, 'The Fatal Five':

1. **Reading the Slides**: Respondents noted that presenters would read slides aloud, or read slides aloud that duplicated the exact information received in the handout. Reading PowerPoint slides is not a strong training technique.
2. **Too Long, Too Much Information**: Too many slides with too many words, too many points, too much data and too didactic in teaching style. The length of the presentation is not necessarily the problem unless the information is boring.
3. **Lack of Interaction**: Presenters who talk for over 30 minutes straight, without stopping to pause or ask if anyone has questions, was a common complaint. Peers over 35 tend to want to learn not just from the presenter but from others in the room.
4. **Lifeless Presenters**: Presenters whose speaking voice is monotonous or who seem to lack interest in their own material were highlighted by many in the survey.
5. **Room/Technical Problems**: Public presenters should anticipate technical problems. While not all technical problems can be avoided, presenters should know how to operate their own equipment and have a backup plan for disseminating the material if necessary. Training rooms that are too cold or too hot were also commonly reported as problematic.

From the same survey, Goodman gleaned 'The Three Most Wanted' components in a presentation:

1. **Interaction**: Nearly 25 percent of all the participants surveyed stated the need for more interaction, either between the speaker and the audience, or among the audience.
2. **Clarity**: Clarity is represented by delivering well organized and concise information, offering three to four well-framed key points that the presenter wants the audience to take away from the presentation.
3. **Enthusiasm**: It is important that presenters are enthusiastic about their topic and convey their enthusiasm and passion to the audience.

It is evident that offline trainings on the topic of online therapy should steer clear of the 'fatal five' components, and, based on the information Goodman presents, a more participant-centered learning approach is warranted. In the traditional model of instruction, participation or interaction among the participants does not occur very much. The didactic approach to teaching and training means that the presenter or trainer does 90 percent of the talking – yet research shows that when there is little interaction among participants, the participants only retain about five percent of the information presented (Vance, 2008).

Typically, interaction does occur at least in Masters level university programs and certainly in counseling programs where the teaching often involves experiential presentation of the material. Increasingly, traditionally taught Masters level university programs about cyberspace and psychology are appearing, such as the one at Dun Laoghaire Institute of Art Design & Technology (IADT) in Ireland and Nottingham Trent University in the UK. In addition, online universities (such as the UK-based Open University) are including online therapy in Foundation Degree trainings which contain interviews with experts on the topic via audio and video within their Virtual Learning Environment (VLE) together with an accompanying textbook.

Of interest and somewhat of a concern to the authors, however, is the lack of courses being taught at the university level in therapy programs across the United States. Furthermore, the Council for Accreditation of Counseling and Related Educational Programs (CACREP) have released their revised 2009 standards and the use of technology in counseling is only referred to once in the 63-page document under Section II: Professional Identity, Item F: 'evidence exists of the use and infusion of technology in program delivery and technology's impact on the counseling profession' (CACREP, 2009: 8). The Council is a large and influential organization to which many graduate level counseling programs look for accreditation. It becomes obvious that teaching counseling students about the use of technology and delivering therapy via technology is not seen as a priority. Certainly, this small provision within the guidelines gives way to programs integrating the use of technology into curriculums but such a small mention of technology's impact on the mental health profession is disconcerting.

Additionally, the Association for Counselor Education and Supervision (ACES), a division of the American Counseling Association (ACA), has established a Code of Ethics for counselor educators and supervisors but no reference is made to technology. ACES have, however, established 'Technical Competencies for Counselor Education', with the latest revision completed in 2007 (Jencius et al., 2007) by the Technology Interest Network. The ACES Technical Competencies address technical competencies for counseling students, from the use of technology equipment to the use of the Internet to conduct research. Included among these competencies is the ability to use technology to develop web pages, group presentations, letters, and reports; to use e-mail; to help clients search for information about careers, employment opportunities, and educational and training opportunities via the Internet; and to evaluate the quality of Internet information. The competencies do not directly address online therapy. However, within the near future, online therapy will likely be addressed by organizations such as CACREP and ACES.

CONFERENCES AND WORKSHOPS

Conference presentations usually last for an hour, and the most basic introduction to the topic would include at least definitions of online work, some trends and statistics, ethical issues, and examples of email and chat room work. Other presentations given worldwide usually include a specific focus on ethics, the therapeutic relationship online, Netiquette, or the future of the profession in light of new technologies such as virtual reality environments. Increasingly, presentations are being sought on boundary-keeping and the professional and personal use of networking sites such as Facebook and Twitter within the profession. These presentations can also be given live online, of course, during a conference where the delegates can be present in one room, or be accessing the conference remotely from around the world, including in Second Life for example.

Longer workshops (such as three hours or more) can include some experiential work, for example exploring fantasies of the unseen client from an email and spotting how this could potentially affect the work in light of assumptions made about them in real life. These workshops can often produce a vibrant discussion and be a useful learning tool before embarking on working online, often at least identifying the need for more in-depth training online before becoming a competent practitioner.

A slightly more intense form of training is a one- or two-day workshop. The latter is a requirement for being a Distance Credentialed Counselor (DCC) in the USA and is described in-depth below. Elsewhere, some e-clinics that offer platforms for online therapy make a one-day training mandatory before therapists can sign-up to work for the service, and many larger organizations such as the UK Inland Revenue Welfare Online Service (now Customs and Excise) stretch this to two days to allow the use of a computer suite for delegates on the second day to put into practice all they have learnt previously with the use of email and live chat rooms.

A sensible agenda for a one-day workshop would include a pre-training information pack about what to expect on the day, and it is often useful for the delegates to complete a questionnaire before the training day to send to the trainer so that the level of understanding and/or experience of online work can be measured. This can be important with group trainings in knowing what learning can be achieved without people being left behind, or more knowledgeable delegates feeling patronized.

The use of pre-training questionnaires also means that the start of the training day itself can contain a group discussion of the participants' hopes and fears about online work as part of the meet and greet session over coffee. This can provide a fascinating insight into current prejudices and preconceptions about online therapy, which the day's content can confirm or dispel. Indeed, conducting a similar session at the close of the day confirms how much myth-busting can be achieved during a one-day workshop.

After the workshop starts, a basic introduction to the various technological methods used for mental health provision online is a good place to start, and this can excite and terrify delegates in equal measure. However, as well as being instructive, it can provide an overview of some of the terms that will be used throughout the day to make the rest of the content more meaningful within the context of cyberspace itself. It is important to debrief after this rather powerful explanation of technology and therapy, as the load of information and demonstrations – particularly of concepts such as group work in virtual environments – can often be overwhelming.

Another important presentation during the workshop, and building on the information disseminated during the first part of the day, is the nuances and specifics of working with text, including Netiquette, acronyms, emoticons, and other Internet conventions. Without being able to cover all the ways of how this takes place in different environments, an overview of the basics is often enough for the trainees to know what Internet communication looks like and to avoid any newbie mistakes. Even basic acronyms such as LOL (Laugh Out Loud) are often mistaken by at least two delegates to mean Lots Of Love, and they will comment about how surprised they were when clients had inserted it into an email or chat.

During the afternoon of a one-day workshop, it is good to allow time for some experiential work. This can take place as a brainstorming around fantasy of the client as mentioned, and this can be extended to being able to spot potential dangers in assessing clients – for instance, providing an email from a client who indicates they may be based in California and so there being particular legal issues in that, or an email from someone whose style of writing indicates that he or she may be younger than actually stated on the intake form. Without facilities for an interactive chat room session such as a computer suite, it is useful to have simulated chats running so that the trainer can explain what may be happening in a session and what the various communications may indicate.

Finally, a one-day workshop should include the group discussing the ethical issues in online therapy, tailored to the kind of service being provided. For instance, this part of a workshop given to an organization who provides the platform for working online will have different ethical concerns to a workshop aimed at a student counseling service.

Basic ethical issues up for discussion include, but are not limited to:

- Competence
- Client inclusions
- Client exclusions
- Cultural issues
- Contracting (informed consent)
- Legal issues
- Clients in crisis
- IT
- Confidentiality
- Limitations
- Training and research matters
- Boundaries
- Supervision
- Regulation.

As stated, it is good to end the day with a plenary session to tie off any loose ends and ensure care of the group. Post-training needs can also easily be catered for online with the provision of a peer support forum for delegates to discuss the day and communicate with the trainer any thoughts or concerns that have occurred to them after the one-day workshop.

DISTANCE CREDENTIALED COUNSELOR (DCC™) TRAINING PROGRAM AND CREDENTIAL

To meet the needs for standards of practice and specialized therapist training, ReadyMinds (www.readyminds.com), in partnership with the Center for Credentialing and Education (CCE) and an affiliate of the National Board of Certified Counselors (NBCC), created a national certification system in the United States. Since 2004, nearly 100 in-person DCC trainings have taken place, training over 1,200 counselors. Of the 1,200 counselors, approximately 500 counselors hold the credential. While primarily practitioners within the US seek the credential, CCE offers the option of foreign degree equivalency, essentially opening the credential to people across the globe.

Requirements to attend the training and receive the DCC credential are as follows (Center for Credentialing and Education, 2003, updated 2009):

Requirements to ATTEND the DCC Training Program include:

1. An earned Masters degree in counseling or an appropriately related field (you do NOT have to possess advanced technology skills).

Requirements to ATTEND the DCC Training Program and OBTAIN the DCC Credential include:

1. An earned Masters degree in counseling or related mental health field from a regionally accredited college or university.
2. Be licensed to practice counseling or a related field in the State or Country in which the candidate resides or works AND/OR be certified in good standing as a National Certified Counselor (NCC).
3. Successful completion of the two-day 15 hour DCC Training Program and the DCC written Training Accountability Requirement (TAR) document.

From inception the DCC training has been facilitated in face-to-face, two-day workshops. The workshops offer continuing education (CE) credit of up to 15 hours for completion of the two-day course. Originally the curriculum coursework was designed and targeted primarily to career counselors but with the growing need for therapists to have specific and related knowledge about the delivery of therapy via technology in the mental health arena, ReadyMinds created an additional curriculum targeting mental health practitioners. While the career and mental health tracks overlap where knowledge and technique are shared, the two separate tracks offer specifics to each area of concentration. The curriculum was designed for mental health therapists offering 20 different training competencies. Ten competencies are taught each day and by the end of the two-day training, the trainee has gained introductory proficiency as an online therapist. Once the training is completed, the trainee completes a Training Accountability Requirement which demonstrates the trainee's ability to assimilate and apply the information.

The face-to-face training includes a combination of teaching methods ranging from didactic to small group activities with learning partners assigned within the class. While each DCC facilitator incorporates his or her own teaching style, the curriculum follows specific key points, utilizing a PowerPoint presentation, a training handbook and various written activities. The trainee is offered written and visual stimulus along with group discussion to incorporate different learning styles. While trainees are not using computers during training for interactive purposes, the facilitator demonstrates chat and video with another facilitator during the actual training. Live access to the Internet allows the facilitator to click to various sites and surf the web through related links and information in the training materials. While a copy of all of the websites used during the training is available to the trainee, another copy is emailed following the training to provide a hyperlinked document for easy manoeuvring. Throughout the two days, as ideas are introduced, the information is repeated within the context of a new competency. At the conclusion of the two days, trainees have not only learned the competencies, they have learned how to begin the process of thinking about how to apply the competencies within their various work settings.

At the time the DCC was first offered, most participants preferred the idea of face-to-face training. Many of the participants even now have rudimentary knowledge of technology. It is not out of place to imagine that many traditionally trained therapists, who have not used technology in their work, may prefer face-to-face interaction. But as the years have passed more and more therapists are requesting the DCC and similar trainings be facilitated online.

Distance Credentialed Counselor (DCC™) Competencies (Nagel et al., 2007)

1. **Distance Credentialed Counselor Work Settings**: Mental health counselors understand how to discuss with both colleagues and clients the various delivery models, work settings, opportunities, advantages, challenges, and professional preparation involved in the delivery of Distance Counseling services within their own specialty area.

2. **History and Current Research**: Mental health counselors understand how to identify and discuss current research/resource that informs Distance Counseling.

3. **Distance Credentialed Counselor Skills**: Mental health counselors understand the skill set necessary to provide distance counseling in an effective and efficient manner.

4. **Informed Consent**: In addition to the typical components of informed consent, mental health counselors understand the importance of informing clients about the advantages and limitations regarding distance counseling.

5. **Client Suitability Screening and Intake**: Mental health counselors understand how to screen clients for suitability in order to deliver appropriately selected methods of distance counseling based on client need.

6. **Modulating Emotions**: Mental health counselors understand how to prepare and educate clients to participate successfully in distance counseling.

7. **Selecting Delivery Methods**: Mental health counselors understand how to use appropriately selected distance counseling delivery methods suited to their

work situations and roles (e.g. telecounseling, asynchronous email/message posting, synchronous digital chat and video-assisted counseling).

8. **Security and Confidentiality Strategies**: Mental health counselors understand how to employ security strategies related to the provision of distance counseling services.

9. **Theory Integration**: Mental health counselors understand how to adapt counseling theory and effective face-to-face counseling techniques for application to distance counseling practice.

10. **Individualized Treatment Plan**: Mental health counselors understand the importance of creating a treatment plan utilizing established protocols.

11. **Between Session Strategies**: Mental health counselors understand how to use technology to help their clients follow up and implement recommendations beyond actual counseling sessions.

12. **Termination and Referral Process**: Mental health counselors know how to bring their clients to closure and help them deal with the termination of the distance counseling process while providing technology-assisted strategies for re-establishing contact if and/or when necessary.

13. **Assessment Instruments**: Mental health counselors understand how to utilize appropriately validated online and offline forms of assessment for clients and to assist them with meaningful interpretation.

14. **Ethical and Legal Issues**: Mental health counselors know how to apply ethical guidelines and standards relevant to distance counseling in their respective fields of practice and know where to find resources on legal guidelines and standards relevant to their specific distance counseling specialties in their states and jurisdiction.

15. **Action Plan Development**: Mental health counselors know how to ethically and responsibly advertise distance counseling services and understand how to incorporate distance counseling services into their existing suite of services.

16. **Online Language and Culture**: Mental health counselors know how to effectively communicate via technology-delivered communications including drafting an initial introductory email, between session emails and treatment summaries.

17. **Consumer Feedback**: Mental health counselors know how to elicit responses from their clients regarding the effectiveness of distance counseling in order to provide continuously improved services.

18. **Cultural Competency**: Mental health counselors understand the importance of cultural competency.

19. **Crisis Intervention**: Mental health counselors know how to facilitate crisis situations that may arise at any point during the therapeutic process, from initial contact to termination.

20. **Education and Supervision**: Mental health counselors understand the need for adequate education, continuing education and supervision throughout the career lifespan.

Clearly, one can ascertain that a two-day training only offers a cursory look into each competency area. Even so, the training prepares the therapist to deliver therapy online and challenges the therapist to continue in the pursuit of knowledge and professional growth.

CONCLUSION

While face-to-face training is a good introduction to working online, it may really only be useful as a brainstorming session amongst novice practitioners to explore the issues, many of which have not even been considered previously, and as an invitation to test the water before embarking on a new strand of one's career, one which may require substantial investment, including further training.

Online training, with its nature of immersion in a non-physical world, is ideal. However, it can also be a lonely training if facilities such as networking and peer-support forums are not utilized, and motivation is lower than for face-to-face trainings. It is also the experience of the authors that because the training is available 24 hours a day, seven days a week, work, family, and other aspects of the offline world can often be given priority rather too easily over the needs of the training. Online training and offline training both hold disadvantages and advantages in their own unique ways.

Having visited the options available to practitioners in training to become an online therapist or use online technologies to enhance their services, we will now attend to some further considerations pertinent to the online therapist in considering online supervision, conducting research online, and group work.

REFERENCES

Balleweg, B. (2000) 'The Interviewing Team: An Exercise for Teaching Assessment and Conceptualization Skills', in M. Ware and D. Johnson (eds), *Handbook of Demonstrations and Activities in the Teaching of Psychology, 2nd edition*, Vol. 3. Philadelphia: Lawrence Erlbaum Associates.

Blatner, A. (2002) 'Role Playing in Education', in *Adam Blatner's Website*. Available at www.blatner.com/adam/pdntbk/rlplayedu.htm [accessed 8 April 2009].

Bloom, J.W. and Waltz, G.R. (2000) *Cybercounselling and Cyberlearning: Strategies and Resources for the Millennium*. Alexandria, VA: ACA/Eric Cass.

CACREP (2009) 'Standards 2009', in *CACREP*. Available at www.cacrep.org/2009 standards.html [accessed 8 April 2009].

Center for Credentialing and Education (2003, updated 2009) 'Information about DCC Training', in *The Center for Credentialing and Education*. Available at www.cce-global.org/credentials-offered/dcctraining [acessed 8 April 2009].

Goodman, A. (2006) *Why Bad Presentations Happen to Good Causes*. Los Angeles, CA: Andy Goodman & Cause Communications. Available at www.agoodmanonline.com/publications/how_bad_presentations_happen/ [accessed 8 April 2009].

Goss, S. and Anthony, K. (2004) 'Ethical and Practical Dimensions of Online Writing Cures', in G. Bolton, S. Howlett, C. Lago and J. Wright (eds), *Writing Cures*. Hove, UK: Brunner-Routledge.

Grauerholz, E. and Copenhaver, S. (1994) 'When the Personal Becomes Problematic: The Ethics of Using Experiential Teaching Methods', in *Teaching Sociology*, 22(4): 319–27.

Jencius, M., Poynton, T.A. and Patrick, P. (2007) 'Technical Competencies for Counselor Education: Recommended Guidelines for Program Development', in *Association for Counselor Education and Supervision*. Available (to members only) at www.aces online.net/documents.asp [accessed 9 April 2009].

Jones, G. and Stokes, A. (2009) *Online Counselling: A Handbook for Practitioners*. Basingstoke: Palgrave Macmillan.

Kay, J.M. (2009) 'Educational Uses in Second Life', in *Second Life in Education Exploring the Educational Uses of Second Life*. Available at http://sleducation. wikispaces.com/educationaluses [accessed 8 April 2009].

Keith-Spiegel, P., Whitley. B.E., Ware Balogh, D., Perkins, D.V. and Wittig, A.F. (2002) *The Ethics of Teaching, 2nd edition*. Philadelphia: Laurence Erlbaum Associates.

Lane, K. (2000) 'Using Actors as "Clients" for an Interviewing Simulation in an Undergraduate Clinical Psychology Course', in M. Ware and D. Johnson (eds), *Handbook of Demonstrations and Activities in the Teaching of Psychology, 2nd edition*, Vol. 3. Philadelphia: Lawrence Erlbaum Associates.

Lehman, R.M. and Berg, R.A. (2007) *147 Tips for Synchronous and Blended Technology Teaching and Learning*. Madison, WI: Atwood Publishing.

Nagel, D.M. (2007) 'Who can Perform Distance Counseling?', in J. Malone, R. Miller and G. Walz (eds), *Distance Counseling: Expanding the Counselor's Reach and Impact*. Ann Arbour, MI: Counseling Outfitters.

Nagel, D.M., Malone, J.F. and Sutherland, J. (2007) *Distance Credentialed Counselor Mental Health Focus Training Handbook*. Internal Proprietary Training Document. Lyndhurst, NJ: ReadyMinds, LLC.

Tyler, J.M. and Sabella, R.A. (2004) *Using Technology to Improve Counseling Practice: A Primer for the 21st Century*. Alexandria, VA: ACA.

Vance, D. (2008) 'Cindy Rae Pautzke – Smashing Pumpkins', in *Connect Business Magazine*. Available at http://connectbiz.com/2008/05/cindy-rae-pautzke/ [accessed 8 April 2009].

Weiss, A.R. (1986) 'Teaching Counseling and Psychotherapy Skills Without Access to a Clinical Population: The Short Interview Method', in *Teaching and Psychology*, 13: 145–7.

Waterhouse, S. (2005) *The Power of eLearning: The Essential Guide for Teaching in the Digital Age*. Upper Saddle River, NJ: Pearson Education, Inc.

Wilkins, P. (2006) 'Professional and Personal Development', in C. Feltham and I. Horton (eds), *The SAGE Handbook of Counselling and Psychotherapy, 2nd edition*. London: Sage.

8
SUPERVISION, RESEARCH AND GROUPS/COUPLES

INTRODUCTION

In this chapter, we shall look at some of the further applications pertinent to the practitioner who has an online presence. Although these further considerations may not be pertinent to all practitioners reading this book, a wider knowledge of the special implications inherent in working online should be useful generally and may be extremely relevant as one's online service grows.

The first consideration – and probably uppermost in the reader's mind, is the need for supervision. There is a general obligation for all counselors, psychotherapists, supervisors and trainers to receive supervision/consultative support independently of any managerial relationships, and for managers, researchers and providers of counseling skills to also assess their needs for supervision (BACP, 2009). Supervisors and managers have a responsibility to maintain and enhance good practice by practitioners, to protect clients from poor practice and to acquire the attitudes, skills and knowledge required by their role (Anthony and Goss, 2009).

In addition, many practitioners translate their online work into academic arenas. The number of Masters theses and PhD research projects is growing as interest in online work grows, and the Internet hosts not only a wealth of information on research papers and articles, but in addition holds many different ways of conducting research, from a single case study to a full meta-analysis project. Conducting research online, whether about online therapy or not, is a topic in itself (Mann and Stewart, 2000; Hooley et al., in press).

Conducting online therapeutic services with more than one person is also a skill, whether with couples, groups or families. Working with multiple clients brings its own particular issues with regard to how it could be conducted, facilitation and boundaries. This can be extremely important in the case of group therapy online, where the possibility of several different cultures being in the room is a reality because of the geographical location being irrelevant.

SUPERVISION

Technology has to some extent been utilized in clinical supervision for several decades, in methods such as transcription, tapes, audio-visual recordings and 'Bug-in-the-ear' and 'Byte-in-the-eye' – an example of one of the first forays into supervision via text is outlined in Stofle and Hamilton (1998). It is important to remember that, just as with online therapy, supervision via technology (cybersupervision, e-supervision, online supervision, e-supervision, etc.) is not a theory or technique, but a conduit to experience a professional and supportive relationship. It can be offered as an adjunct to a face-to-face relationship, often utilizing technologies such as the telephone, videoconferencing or virtual reality as well as the online methods under discussion here, to deliver services. Alternatively, practitioners may choose to conduct the relationship solely via the methods used to conduct the therapeutic relationship itself. Thus, if a practitioner uses chat sessions plus interim email with a client, the supervisory relationship reflects this.

There is ongoing debate as to whether online supervision is a requirement of being an online counselor. The Association for Counselling and Therapy Online (www.acto-uk.org) recommends this (and Jones and Stokes (2009) do not recommend online supervision for face-to-face work), but there is also an argument for an offline supervisor having a more objective view of the process of the work and being less concerned with the nuances of the modality and how that may be affecting the therapeutic input. Conversely, online supervision could be extremely useful for the face-to-face therapist who finds they have problems gaining access to a face-to-face supervisor, as Jones and Stokes also acknowledge. As the 2009 BACP Guidelines state:

> Practitioners and organisations must consider carefully how they may best receive supervision for their online practice (face-to-face or online), and ensure that the supervisor is experienced and trained in online work and has a full understanding of the issues and ethical concerns inherent in it. Practitioners must also consider the issues surrounding client consent, confidentiality and data protection/storage when using online supervision, and encryption packages and privacy tools are again essential. (Anthony and Goss, 2009: 6)

Note should also be taken regarding the location of the supervisor and supervisee, and whether the qualifications of the former are suitable and equivalent enough to the requirement of the country the latter is resident in. Supervisors also need to be aware of the professional and legal requirement of the supervisee if she or he is located in a different country. Practitioners may contract to make further arrangements to be satisfied of each other's identity before the session actually begins, possibly by the use of code words, if cases are particularly sensitive with regard to the session being stored verbatim and in light of the possibility of work being subpoenaed.

Email

Using email for supervision is not a new concept. Myrick and Sabella (1995) discussed the use of email for supervision as early as 1995. Even in a clinical face-to-face relationship for supervision, the parties usually use email casually for scheduling, case staffing and offering feedback. Adjunct email between sessions may be used by the supervisee as a way of processing supervisory material or informing the supervisor of progress post supervision session. Additional information and relevant material, such as articles, can be emailed as part of the supervision process. Email is also extremely useful for checking in with the supervisee who is handling a particularly difficult clinical case, to offer extra or wider support and encouragement.

The use of email has become so common that most people understand email etiquette, although training in this is still encouraged to avoid even the most basic of misunderstandings creating a flame war and leading to a breakdown in the supervisory relationship. Contracts can clearly state how the parties should handle such misunderstandings (and in addition how disagreements about client care itself should be addressed). All aspects of email communication should be considered. From the email subject line to the body of the email to the email closure, each part of the email has the potential to carry expression and meaning. Conveying empathy and emotion through email text using emoticons, parenthetical expression and quoted text is every bit as important in a clinical relationship as they are in the therapeutic relationship.

Supervisors may construct emails differently and with different purposes depending from which theoretical orientation the supervisor is operating. Email is akin to letter writing in that both parties have a chance to be reflective and think through thoughts and suppositions during the composition. Because email is an asynchronous form of communication, an immediate response should not be expected. Contracting is vital, with both parties being absolutely clear as to when responses are to be read (as opposed to when they are sent), and how frequently. Both parties should also be open to the flexibility of these arrangements, with the possibility of exchanges becoming less frequent over time due to necessity and client load. Supervisors have an opportunity to posit questions to the supervisee and the supervisee can answer with researched or spontaneous thought. There is also room for emergency 'one-off' exchanges for supervision in cases of crisis consultation being needed outside of a supervisory contract.

Forums and listservs

Bulletin boards and forums are similar in set up, and are particularly useful for group supervision and are usually hosted on a web page wherein parties can log in using a user name and password. The moderator or facilitator of the forum can determine who has access to the forum and offer a pre-screening/registration process or allow individuals to sign up at will. Listservs are similarly moderated. While forums are viewed by topic and each topic may have a thread of responses, listservs are generally delivered as an email response or as a group of responses at the end of the day, as noted in the Introduction. Preferences for either forums or listservs vary, and it is useful for the parties to discuss this preference before the process commences, as use of a non-preferred format often results in drop-off of participants very quickly. Forums and listservs can be useful to the clinical supervision process offering asynchronous group supervision or peer consultation. A forum can be set up to be moderated by a clinical supervisor who may choose to 'screen' each post before allowing the post to appear on the forum, which is particularly useful if the process of anonymizing client material starts being forgotten or treated casually. The supervisor may alternatively allow postings by supervisees without prior screening and intercede as necessary to redirect or correct. Most listservs have fewer moderator features. In either case, the group rules can stipulate what constitutes inappropriate behavior, and what subsequent sanctions are available to the facilitator if there is a breach of group rules.

It should be noted that with email and forums, just as in more general arenas, the supervisee might have the opportunity to state frankly what is on his or her mind, as the asynchronous nature allows for emotional venting. The emotion can be released and the writer of the message can simply 'walk away' with no expectation of an immediate response, which Munro (2002) accurately refers to as 'emotional hit and run'. The message may seem particularly critical or may appear to have been written without forethought. It is important that the supervisor has the opportunity to engage the supervisee in processing this material, either before the message is allowed to be viewed by others or as part of the group supervision process.

Suler (2001) provides a handy 10-point checklist of 'rules' for being part of an online supervisory group. These include understanding how different members pace their responses (which may be different to one's own pace), precision in quoting previous text, letting the group know of absences, and letting the group know of concerns. Of particular interest is the use of a 'process thread' – a separate channel through which members of a group can objectively look at the process of the group in the event of misunderstandings, confusions, or disagreements.

IM and chat

Utilizing Instant Messaging and chat is an effective way to process clinical supervision issues, again either as a stand-alone experience or as adjunct to face-to-face supervision and/or other technology delivery methods. Supervisors can schedule formal sessions with supervisees weekly or fortnightly, replicating the typical clinical supervision hour. Supervisors who are offering direction and supervision in an agency setting may choose to be available for immediate contact, using symbols that are available in most chat programs to signify availability (e.g. Available, Away, Busy, Do Not Disturb). Boundaries for impromptu contact should be established between the supervisor and supervisee so that a clear understanding exists regarding the need for immediate contact. Supervisees, with the proper established boundaries, may experience comfort knowing their supervisor is accessible regardless of the supervisee's intent or need to make immediate contact.

Many supervisees like to email case summaries and an agenda before the chat session starts, to allow best use of the time scheduled to be online together. In this way, the focus can remain on the supervisory issue rather than the time being taken up explaining the case material within the session.

The tendency for the supervisee to use text for emotional venting as with asynchronous forms of communication is less likely in chat. Still, the lack of visual and auditory cues may prompt a supervisee to state information of a personal nature that is not relevant or that might be more detailed than he or she might ordinarily share in a face-to-face session. The supervisor should be aware of this possibility and assist the supervisee in remaining focused on issues pertaining to clients and the therapeutic work setting.

Similar to the use of phone, IM/chat can differ from face-to-face sessions in terms of pacing and moments of silence. While many IM/chat programs offer a prompt that alerts the person that a response is forthcoming (e.g. *Jane is typing a response…*) other programmes do not offer a textual cue to alert that the person is typing. Silences should be expected and, with proper pacing, addressed. In the context of a therapeutic chat session, the supervisee might benefit from the use of emotional bracketing to describe to the supervisor what feelings have been evoked during the clinical supervision session.

General points

All these methods of delivery need consideration by the parties as to how records will be stored, both electronically (hard-drive, external drive, or held on a server) and print versions and for how long, particularly with regard to transcript material. Appropriate disposal of records and transcripts should also be considered carefully. Alongside these considerations, the benefit of having a transcript of supervision sessions to refer to could also be recognized as being convenient in possibly usurping the need to take notes (Stokes, 2006). In addition, as with online therapy, text-based communication for the purposes of case consultation, peer supervision or clinical supervision should be encrypted, even if proper precautions have been taken to properly blind the record from information that may identify the client (Nagel, et al., in press).

Post-supervision qualification training in online supervision is recommended. Courses should encompass the basics of online therapy itself and the supervisory module(s) could be an adjunct to them.

Care should be taken with the possibility of developing dual relationships in the light of social and professional networking sites. While professional relationships flourish in cyberspace via networking, both supervisor and supervisee carry a risk of their professional relationship becoming blurred into a friendship that could affect the clinical supervision when brought into a more formal arena.

An interesting debate in online (or offline) supervision is that of the appropriateness or otherwise of the supervisee being able to point their supervisor to web-based content maintained by the client in order to illustrate the case being presented in supervision (Fenichel, 2003). This could be troubling messages, artwork, blogs or forum posts. Indeed, researching one's clients personally outside of the therapeutic remit (for example Googling them) may be considered a breach of privacy, and this can apply to supervisors and supervisees equally, and certainly in the case of sharing the client's online life with others for the purpose of supervision.

Online supervision, while not exactly in its infancy, is still a new phenomenon. Few guidelines exist, and very little empirical research has been conducted, particularly with regard to text-based supervision, although fascinating exploratory qualitative studies are available, such as the work of the ISMHO Case Study Group (Fenichel and Suler, 2000). However, just as with online therapy itself, practitioners are seeking out online professional services for supervision, and equally, those able to meet the need are providing those services. Supervision has a consumer base, and the Internet is a cost-effective and convenient way of working.

RESEARCH (written with Stephen Goss)

As a general rule, practitioners are 'required to keep abreast of research and opinion in the field of online therapy, and membership of an organization that is dedicated to the understanding and development of online mental health research and services is recommended' (Anthony and Goss, 2009: 5). Certainly, there is a wealth of means by which practitioners can keep up-to-date with research, through online libraries and indexes of research or academic publications. There is also an increasing number of organizations that include research at least nominally as part of their remit.

However, there is a wider picture for practitioners in any field of therapy for whom awareness of how to conduct research online is relevant; BACP (2009: 5) also notes that 'regularly monitoring and reviewing one's work is essential to main-taining one's practice'. At minimum, practitioners should be sufficiently aware of the issues to be critical consumers of research reports.

Both quantitative and qualitative research methods bring additional issues when transferred to the online environment. The Internet has been used as an environment for social, cultural and psychological research for some time (Bosnjak et al., 2001). Counseling, psychotherapy and mental health issues were present relatively early in this process (see Walther and Burgoon, 1992) and continue to develop, offering prac-titioners an increasingly useful evidence base for their work (see Rochlen et al., 2004).

However, some caution is necessary. A number of authors have argued that while the quantity of data that can be collected online, and the speed with which it can be offered, can provide what might appear to be an appealing option for researchers, we should take care to ensure that 'cheap entry costs and glowing attractiveness of Internet fieldwork do not result in cowboy research' (Dodd, 1998). Survey data, espe-cially, is only useful if it represents the wider population under discussion, and ensur-ing representative sampling methods can be problematic, certainly unless the population under consideration is purely the online community, although even there issues of wider generalizability can remain. Thus, gaining a clear picture of the group one intends to investigate is all the more important in online research lest the data gathered pertain only to a portion of the population under discussion. It is little use investigating, say, differences between male and female experiences of online rela-tionships, if one does not begin with reliable information on the proportions of men and women who are active online.

There are also concerns about whether responding to a research study online will give different data than if the same studies were conducted offline, but that is not to say that online research is necessarily unreliable. Indeed, it is entirely possible for research over the Internet to match studies carried out offline and, where careful control and design is achieved, response rates and the characteristics of those who do or do not respond have been found to be equivalent in at least some studies (Reynolds and Stiles, 2007). The point to note is that research must be carefully designed to account for the effects of computer mediated interaction. A 'digital divide' separates researchers from potential respondents who either do not have Internet access at all or who choose to use it for highly specific purposes, potentially excluding whole sections of society, especially older age groups, socially disadvantaged people or those outwith Westernized societies.

There is no doubt that effects such as disinhibition may also alter responses to certain questions, especially on the highly personal matters often associated with therapy. Greater honesty from respondents is generally highly desirable but may reduce the comparability of online findings with those obtained offline and such differences must be accounted for with a reasonable degree of certainty. The degree of technical competence required to respond to online research studies can also be an issue, potentially excluding those with lower opportunity or ability to comfortably operate the platform used in a given study (Illingworth, 2001; O'Connor and Madge, 2001) suggesting that online researchers should pay particular attention to ensuring that respondents' tasks are as simple and straightforward as possible, to an extent greater than that required of offline studies.

Nonetheless, such cautions should not obscure the positive advantages offered by online methods. These have been identified by Madge et al. (2006) as including: the ability to contact geographically dispersed populations (of special importance for international research); facilitating contact with groups who are otherwise difficult to reach and may thus be under-represented in offline studies, such as, for example, those who are disabled or in prison or in hospital; significant potential savings in costs through reduced travel or venue costs; the rapid supply of data in digital form (ready transcribed interview data from chat or email exchanges); and reductions in the effect the interviewer may have on their respondent, potentially rendering at least some online data *more* reliable than that gathered through other means. Some data processing can also be automated, further reducing the time and cost requirements for conducting studies. Even where the experience under investigation took place offline, online studies can still offer all these advantages. Moreover, where a population under scrutiny is closely defined and likely to have Internet access and the given level of technical competence required, as would probably be the case in most studies of clients of online therapy, a number of the difficulties recede. With careful interpretation and appropriate caution when comparing findings with offline studies, disinhibition can also be a positive boon. Poster (1995: 90) points out 'without visual clues about gender, age, ethnicity and social status conversations open up in directions which might otherwise be avoided ... with little inhibition and dialogues flourish and develop quickly'.

Distinct Internet methodologies have also evolved, such as 'netnography' (Kozinets, 1998; Langer and Beckman, 2005), an evolution of the ethnographic methods familiar to many social and psychological science investigators. For example, it is possible for studies to include participant-observation of content and behavior in email lists or exchanges, discussion groups, or specialist forums or professional/social networking services. A researcher might examine video exchanges (Wesch, 2008) or the written record afforded by chat or email therapy exchanges with counseling clients. Indeed, access to the complete verbatim records offered by online therapy is one of the distinct advantages of conducting research into therapeutic process and outcomes online. Typically, face-to-face therapy at least requires transcription of counselor–client interactions, often a laborious, time consuming, and therefore costly, research task in qualitative studies.

Madge et al. (2006) emphasize that use of interviewing techniques, focus groups and similar methods in research traditionally 'rely heavily on the use of visual and physical clues and pointers in order to build rapport and gain the trust of the interviewee'. In the online environment even such basic skills must be radically re-imagined given that many of the interpersonal tools used face-to-face to develop rapport are absent. Familiar though many of the changes required may be to an experienced online therapist, when it comes to research it should also be borne in mind that 'a stranger wanting to do academic research into online communities is often viewed as an unwelcome arbitrary intrusion' (Paccagnella, 1997: para 16). It is vital for researchers using any technique, especially any approach that requires interaction with participants, like interviewing, first to gain insights into the culture and communication style of the environment being researched, mastering the culture and communication styles exhibited by their intended participants. There are a number of specific techniques that can help researchers, and their respondents, establish a productive relationship. For example, creating a web page with information including brief biographical information, even photographs, and background detail to the study so that participants can gain extra knowledge about the interviewer and can establish at least some relationship prior to the start of the research itself. Using personal and professional similarities or insider status can encourage identification and sharing one's profile data can assist in encouraging others to do so too. Managing online research groups can be challenging even for experienced researchers, as discussed in the next section.

Ethical issues raised by online research tend to be similar to those in offline studies, with a few additional complexities. For example, researchers may have more difficulty determining whether the data being researched is public (like an open meeting), private (like a therapy session) or somewhere in between (like a café or bar). The writer's intention should generally be the guiding factor (do they mean their words to be treated like published material in a book like material in public areas of many websites, or is it intended for a more limited audience like a listserv discussion or social network?) There are also issues relating to the apparent anonymity that many Internet users may have assumed. Many will be happy to be known within their own community but without necessarily wanting their words to be used more widely. In all such situations, obtaining properly informed consent is especially important and where it is not available, such as where the identity of respondents cannot be verified, researchers should take particular care. Just as with any provision of therapy online, privacy must be protected, for example through encryption and careful data storage, processing and reporting.

COUPLE, GROUP AND FAMILY WORK ONLINE

There are various ways of offering multiple participant services online, just as there are with individual therapy services. In the early days, and before the Web appeared in its current format, the first text-based communities took the form of Usenet bulletin boards, called 'news groups', and peer support via anything with the suffix 'alt.support' attracted thousands of participants. There is still a searchable archive of more than 700 million Usenet postings from a period covering more than 20 years (http://groups.google.com).

The platforms used for conducting multi-occupancy services are the same as for other services, with the semantic exception of multi-occupant IMs being a chat room. Therefore forums, chat rooms and email listservs all apply for group work, as previously discussed with reference to individual therapy.

Couple therapy

One of the most attractive aspects of couple therapy online is that it combines a safe space for two people to interact with each other (and the therapist) with the positive benefits of disinhibition, allowing them the freedom to talk freely where face-to-face communication is difficult. Derrig-Palumbo and Zeine (2005) point out that the pace of the therapy is much more considerate of the other person as one has to wait for the other to finish inputting text. Considering, typing and then witnessing the communication also helps the couple to take responsibility for their words and actions. If facilitated well by the therapist, cross-talking and interruptions are minimized.

In using chat rooms for the therapy, each partner may be at different locations to take part, or couples can take turns at the same keyboard on one terminal. The latter option could be quite complicated and frustrating, with waiting for one's turn creating tension and with the disinhibition being disrupted as the other party sees what the partner is typing. This may be lessened by the online therapy being preceded by one or two face-to-face sessions, still using a computer, which allows the therapist to see the interaction between them and how this may affect the process when needing to use a shared computer to interface without the therapist in the room. A further stage in this process is for the couple to then make the move to separate locations to continue the work and take advantage of the disinhibition effect to release emotions which had been suppressed, before the therapist brings them back to working at the same computer.

If the couple therapy takes place face-to-face, Derrig-Palumbo and Zeine (2005) recommend that couples communicate via email or chat between sessions if there is a block in the therapeutic process. The freedom of expression can help the flow of communication without the interruptions that can happen in a face-to-face session and minimizes the negative effect of physical facial reactions to what is being discussed. The couple can work through problems via healthy, intimate communication via text, which can be brought into the face-to-face session to practice translating this into interactive personal communication.

Couple therapy may also occur utilizing email exchanges. In this manner, the partners each take turns emailing the therapist. The therapist then responds openly in an email to both partners addressing all concerns. Email exchanges continue in this manner with the goal of consensus between the partners.

Jencius and Sager provided an overview of marriage and family counseling in cyberspace in 2001, including ethical guideline development, and pointing out that although guidelines for counseling in cyberspace in general were beginning to emerge and that most of the issues inherent in that were applicable to this client group, there was no specific mention of couple therapy. However, by 2005, the International Association for Marriage and Family Counselors had included a clause to specify work via technological intervention:

> Marriage and family counselors maintain ethical and effective practices as they address the benefits and limitations of technological innovations and cultural changes. Counseling may be conducted or assisted by telephones, computer hardware and software, and other communication technologies. Technology-assisted distance counseling services may expand the scope and influence of marriage and family counseling. However, counselors are responsible for developing competencies in the use of new technologies and safeguarding private and confidential information. (IAMFC, 2005: 6–7)

The BACP Guidelines make a point of highlighting that practitioners should be aware of the additional complexities of working with couples in this way and ensure they are properly trained and prepared for it.

Family therapy

Online family therapy works well because of the familiarity of the younger members with the technology being used, which often makes them feel more included and accepted into the dynamics of the therapy process itself. This includes reducing the possibility of participants being talked over or feeling discounted, as the communication is there in black and white, permanently, and can be referred back to by the therapist if it seems to have been ignored by the other members of the group.

Derrig-Palumbo and Zeine (2005) feel that using chat for these sessions can be limiting due to the number of people taking part and recommend the inclusion of video so that the therapist can observe voice patterns and non-verbal behavior, but chat should not be excluded because of this, particularly if being used as an adjunct to face-to-face sessions or if members of the family are geographically spread out. It can also be extremely useful when the original nuclear family is broken and new relationships have been formed with step-parents or siblings that affect relationships – whether positively or negatively – with the biological members of the original family (or vice versa). Page et al. (2000) set up support groups in the virtual environment, The Palace (www.thepalace.com), and noted that graphical icons that pictorially represented family members were useful. Using online asynchronous tools can also fit neatly into the different work or school patterns of the various family members (King et al., 1998), and the delayed response time allows the client to fully digest and consider what has been said.

Group therapy

Online modalities have opened up groupwork completely, not least because members of a group can contribute and take part from anywhere in the world. Again – with the exception of one-to-one Instant Messaging – email, listservs, forums, and chat rooms can all be used to facilitate groups. There are a myriad of online support groups evidenced by the original .alt newsgroups as mentioned previously, but it is the therapist-facilitated groups that we will concentrate on here.

Therapist-led online groups should not involve the anonymity that many support groups find useful (or detrimental) in being able to freely communicate without fear of identification. Intake procedures should be as strict as for any embarkation on a therapeutic process, but with particular regard to the rules of participation between group members. Colon and Friedman (2003) cite the case of a young man wishing to take part in their cancer support group, but whose non-cancer related needs, which included self-harm, suicidal ideation and a longstanding history of depression were too great for him to be able to focus sufficiently on the purpose of the group. The assessment procedure showed that he did not have the ability to maintain the boundaries necessary to take part in such a group.

Facilitation of online groups can be difficult, and it is important for the facilitator to decide beforehand how much time he or she is able and willing to devote to the group, in being available, reading the posts, moderating them as necessary and responding, and communicating (if at all) with the group members outside of the group (via email or other 'back channel' communication). Alternatively, in the case of synchronous methods, the frequency and length of the group sessions must be decided. Consideration is also needed of how to handle emergencies and management issues with regards to flames and flame wars being instigated through misunderstandings, which can happen very quickly in a group, especially where the posts aren't moderated before being made public.

Yalom and Meszcz (2005) state that in face-to-face work, an ideal group size may be seven or eight members with a range of five to 10. Barak and Wander-Schwartz (1999) conducted brief group therapy in chat rooms with a group size of seven. However, Nagel (2009) suggests three to six with an optimum size of four members for a synchronous group, and commentators agree. Allowing for attrition, a maximum number of six participants may result in a consistent number of three to five. She acknowledges that asynchronous communication offers an opportunity for more members, and that two facilitators, regardless of the delivery method, is always optimal but not necessarily practical.

Asynchronous modalities allow for much longer, and therefore possibly much richer, posts. In these groups, the facilitator needs to listen to the dynamics of the group with regard to how often responses are sent, possible apparently absent members (lurkers), frequent contributors who may dominate the group, and the tone of voice used in usual posts so that changes in mood can be picked up and acted upon if the therapist feels a member needs additional care. Colon and Friedman (2003) identify these changes as, for example, the sudden use of fragmented sentences or unusual grammatical errors possibly indicating when members are anxious, depressed or angry. Having a verbatim transcript of the group therapy can often be invaluable, not only from a research or process analysis point of view but also in ensuring members' safety. When face-to-face, a mood change can be identified by a change in physical presence (slumped shoulders, weariness, etc.), the online group therapist has only the written word to recognize this mood change, which can be confirmed by comparison of previous posts and sentence structure or tone of content.

The therapist must also be very aware of his or her own contributions to the group. Too many posts can be intrusive, and too few can make the group feel neglected – often leading to members dropping out. This also applies to the group members' participation, in that the perceived absence of others leads to a lack of motivation to contribute regularly or at all. The therapist needs dedicated skills to keep the group going while allowing the group process to take place, particularly in light of the focus of the group being anxiety, depression or physical illness. Responses (or lack of them) to members can often make or break a group, but the therapist should not take responsibility for maintaining this alone (dominating the group and leading members to consider their contributions unnecessary) but encourage the group dynamic to be vibrant.

The management of conflict in a group also needs refined skills on the part of the therapist, particularly in the case of a forum or listserv where posts are not modified. Non-moderated forums are less work for the therapist from an administrative point-of-view, and also allow the group to function 24 hours a day rather than being restricted to the therapist's own time zone. However, this does include the possibility of flame wars flaring up very rapidly – even overnight – without management of them by the facilitator. The conflict between members (including between members and the therapist) needs to be addressed and mediated before it can escalate, and Colon and Friedman (2003) again give a good case study of how this can happen as the members of their cancer support group look to the 'group leader' to deal with conflict and help members work towards a resolution, or, in this case, accept that this is not possible and that the member wishes to leave the group because of the conflict.

Termination of the group also needs careful consideration, and often includes a review of the process from the therapist. As the ending approaches, members can take the opportunity to say goodbye and give feedback to the therapist about their experience. The group, although closed, may be left as an archive for members to revisit which often allows a holding capacity for the member post-therapy, to re-experience the support that occurred during the therapeutic process itself.

CONCLUSION

Whether practitioners wish to work online or not, it is extremely important that they have a basic knowledge and familiarity with the online lives that their supervisees, and their supervisee's clients, could live (Anthony, 2001, for example). Without an understanding of the changing face of communication online and the possible negative affects this can have on lives, such as the potential effects of cyberinfidelity or cyberbullying, supervisors will not be able to work competently in the field of online therapy, to the detriment of their supervisee and indeed the clients of the supervisee. This is also the case for traditional supervision and clients in traditional therapy.

Online research offers exciting opportunities. While online studies are not a replacement for offline approaches and must not be treated as a 'quick fix' for the problems of researchers, where carefully used with proper attention to ethical and methodological issues, they can offer a valuable route by which we can expand our knowledge and evidence base regarding online therapy. Indeed, it is quite possible for online therapists to build in evaluation, or other kinds of investigation of their work, by inclusion of simple psychometrics and/or qualitative evidence gathering as a routine part of their work. Should more practitioners take steps to do so, the evidence base available for online therapeutic services would be far better developed than is currently the case. Imagine what expansion of our understanding of the phenomenon of online therapy could be achieved if all the potential for evidence gathering offered by online working were taken up.

Group work online carries its own peculiarities, and certainly its own skills, in managing a couple, family or group online. Group work also remains the most under-researched and undiscussed client group, which would indicate its complexities and the nature of the feat for the practitioner in taking on group work online. However, with skill and an appropriate formation of how the modality could work best for any couple or group, it can be a very effective and dynamic way of working, offering benefit to the clients and satisfaction for the therapist, albeit usually tinged with sadness at closure, just as with face-to-face work.

Having considered these three further considerations of online work, we can turn to the future of online therapy in Chapter 9, and our concluding thoughts.

REFERENCES

Anthony, K. (2001) 'Online Relationships and Cyberinfidelity', in *Counselling*, 12(9): 38–9. Available at www.kateanthony.co.uk [accessed 8 April 2009].

Anthony, K. and Goss, S. (2009) *Guidelines for Online Counselling and Psychotherapy, Including Guidelines for Online Supervision, 3rd edition*. Lutterworth: BACP.

BACP (2009) *Ethical Framework for Good Practice in Counselling and Psychotherapy*. Lutterworth: BACP.

Barak, A. and Wander-Schwartz, M. (1999) 'Empirical Evaluation of Brief Group Therapy Through an Internet Chat Room', in *construct.haifa.ac.il*. Available at http://construct.haifa.ac.il/~azy/cherapy.htm [accessed 9 February 2009].

Bosnjak, M., Tuten, T.L. and Bandilla, W. (2001) 'Participation in Web Surveys: a Typology', in *ZUMA Nachrichten*, 48: 7–17.

Colon, Y. and Friedman, B. (2003) 'Conducting Group Therapy Online', in S. Goss and K. Anthony (eds), *Technology in Counselling and Psychotherapy: A Practitioner's Guide*. Basingstoke, UK: Palgrave Macmillan.

Derrig-Palumbo, K. and Zeine, F. (2005) *Online Therapy: A Therapist's Guide to Expanding Your Practice*. New York: Norton.

Dodd, J. (1998) 'Market Research on the Internet – Threat or Opportunity?', in *Marketing and Research Today*, 26(1): 60–6.

Fenichel, M. (2003) 'The Supervisory Relationship Online', in S. Goss and K. Anthony (eds), *Technology in Counselling and Psychotherapy: A Practitioner's Guide*. Basingstoke, UK: Palgrave.

Fenichel, M. and Suler, J. (2000) 'The Online Clinical Case Study Group of the International Society for Mental Health Online: A Report from the Millennium Group', in *ISMHO*. Available at www.ismho.org/rpt_millenium_grp.asp [accessed 8 April 2009].

Hooley, T., Wellens, J., Madge, C. and Goss, S. (in press) 'Using Online Methods for Counselling and Psychotherapy Research', in K. Anthony and D.M. Nagel (eds), *Mental Health and the Impact of Technological Development*. Springfield, IL: Charles Thomas Publishing.

IAMFC (2005) 'Ethical Code of the International Association of Marriage and Family Counselors (IAMFC)', in *International Association of Marriage and Family Counselors*. Available at www.iamfc.com/revised_ethical_codes.doc [accessed 8 April 2009].

Illingworth, N. (2001) 'The Internet Matters: Exploring the Use of the Internet as a Research Tool', in *Sociological Research Online*, 6(2). Available at www.socresonline.org.uk/6/2/illingworth.html [accessed 8 April 2009].

Jencius, M. and Sager, D.E. (2001) 'The Practice of Marriage and Family Counseling in Cyberspace', in *The Family Journal*, 9(3): 295–301.

Jones, G. and Stokes, A. (2009) *Online Counselling: A Handbook for Practitioners*. Basingstoke: Palgrave Macmillan.

King, S.A., Engi, S. and Poulos, S.T. (1998) 'Using the Internet to Assist Family Therapy', in *British Journal of Guidance and Counselling*, 26(1): 43–52.

Kozinets, R.V. (1998) 'On Netnography: Initial Reflections on Consumer Investigations of Cyberculture', in *Advances in Consumer Research*, 25(1): 366–71.

Langer, R. and Beckman, S. (2005) 'Sensitive Research Topics: Netnography Revisited', in *Qualitative Market Research: An International Journal*, 8(2): 189–203.

Madge, C., O'Connor, H., Wellens, J., Hooley, T. and Shaw R. (2006) *Exploring Online Research Methods in a Virtual Training Environment*. Available at www.geog.le.ac.uk/orm [accessed 8 April 2009].

Mann, C. and Stewart, F. (2000) *Internet Communication and Qualitative Research – A Handbook for Researching Online*. London: Sage.

Munro, K. (2002) 'Conflict in Cyberspace: How to Resolve Conflict Online', in *KaliMunro.com*. Available at www.kalimunro.com/article_conflict_online.html [accessed 8 April 2009].

Myrick, R.D. and Sabella, R.A. (1995) 'Cyberspace: New Place for Counselor Supervision', in *Elementary School Guidance and Counseling*, 30(1): 35–44.

Nagel, D.M. (2009) 'Group Therapy Online – Optimum Group Size?', in *Online Therapy Institute*. Available at http://www.onlinetherapyinstituteblog.com/?p=256 [accessed 8 April 2009].

Nagel, D.M., Goss, S. and Anthony, K. (in press) 'The Use of Technology in Supervision', in N. Pelling, J. Barletta and P. Armstrong (eds), *The Practice of Supervision*. Bowen Hills, QLD: Australian Academic Press.

O'Connor, H. and Madge, C. (2001) 'Cyber-mothers: Online Synchronous Interviewing using Conferencing Software', in *Sociological Research Online*, 5(4). Available at www.socresonline.org.uk/5/4/o'connor.html [accessed 8 April 2009].

Paccagnella, (1997) 'Getting the Seats of Your Pants Dirty: Strategies for Ethnographic Research on Virtual Communities', in *Journal of Computer-Mediated Communication*, 3(1). Available at http://jcmc.indiana.edu/vol3/issue1/paccagnella.html [accessed 8 April 2009].

Page, B.J., Delmonico, D.L., Walsh, J.L., Amoreaux, N.A., Danninhirsh, C., Thompson, R.S., Ingram, A.I. and Evans, A.D. (2000) 'Setting Up Online Support Groups using The Palace Software', in *Journal for Specialists in Group Work*, 25(2): 133–45.

Poster, M. (1995) 'Postmodern Virtualities', in M. Fetherstone and R. Burrows (eds), *Cyberspace/Cyberbodies/Cyberpunk: Cultures of Technological Embodiment*. London: Sage.

Reynolds, D. and Stiles, W. (2007) 'Online Data Collection for Psychotherapy Process Research', in *Cyberpsychology and Behavior*, 10(1): 92–9.

Rochlen, A., Zack, J. and Spayer, C. (2004) 'Online Therapy: Review of Relevant Definitions, Debates and Current Empirical Support', in *Journal of Clinical Psychology*, 60(3): 269–83.

Stofle, G. and Hamilton, S. (1998) 'Online Supervision', in *The New Social Worker*, 5(1). Available at www.socialworker.com/onlinesu.htm [accessed 8 April 2009].

Stokes, A. (2006) 'Supervision in Cyberspace', in *Counselling at Work*, Winter: 5–7. Available at www.counsellingatwork.org.uk/journal_pdf/acw_winter06_b.pdf [accessed 8 April 2009].

Suler, J. (2001) 'The Online Clinical Case Study Group: An Email Model', in *CyberPsychology and Behavior*, 4(6): 711–22.

Walther, J.B. and Burgoon, J.K. (1992) 'Relational Communication in Computer-mediated Interaction', in *Human Communication Research*, 19(1): 50–88.

Wesch, M. (2008) 'An Anthropological Introduction to YouTube', in *You Tube*. Available at http://uk.youtube.com/watch?v=TPAO-lZ4_hU [accessed 8 April 2009].

Yalom, I.D. and Meszcz, M. (2005) *The Theory and Practice of Group Psychotherapy, 5th edition*. New York: Basic Books.

9
A LOOK TO THE FUTURE AND CONCLUDING THOUGHTS

INTRODUCTION

Traditional methods of delivering therapy will not be replaced. However, what is exciting about the use of technology in therapy is the variation and flexibility it offers us in extending and adapting traditional face-to-face therapy. This chapter discusses just some of the exciting developments in the field, from the familiar types of delivery such as the landline telephone, to the more innovative developments such as virtual reality environments and the concept of Web 2.0 and what that may mean for the profession.

In 2003, Goss and Anthony noted how the acceleration of developments in technology constantly bring new ideas to the profession in providing a more efficient and accessible way of delivering and receiving mental health services. They also noted that technology facilitates communication but does not create it. With the development of social and professional networking in particular, this holds more truth than could have been predicted in that the next incarnation of the Internet – and indeed those beyond the next – holds this kernel of truth as its central tenet. Communication between human beings has never been easier, to the point at which we can know what a complete stranger (and one we are never likely to meet face-to-face) is doing from one minute to the next via networking sites such as Twitter and Facebook, not only by logging into a website but by push technology to a mobile or cell phone device. These often strangely compelling methods of communication can be seen as facilitating a fundamental aspect of human nature – reaching out to one another. Facilitation does not mean creation, however.

So in concluding this book, we shall visit some of the other technologies that facilitate the delivery of mental health assistance, with both their advantages and disadvantages.

TELEPHONE THERAPY

It is perhaps surprising to think that telephone counseling has been recognized for over 40 years, and yet it was only as recently as 2006 that UK Guidelines were published by the country's main organization, five years after the original BACP Guidelines for online work and a year after the 2nd edition of the same. Guidelines were published in 1999 for helpline work by the Telephone Helplines Association (THA, 1999), with additional information for 'non-voice channels' such as email several years later (THA, 2007). However, for contracted therapy (rather than helplines), the use of telephones is a useful technological tool for conducting a therapeutic relationship, and increasingly becomes another modality within a suite of services. Key skills identified by Logan and Trench (2007) include:

- Highly developed listening and communication skills
- Assessment and referral skills
- Achieving positive outcomes
- Working with ethical issues
- Working with boundary issues (in light of easier access to the therapist)
- Being able to handle 'difficult' calls
- Knowing how to open and close calls.

Essentially, their point is that with telephone counseling, as in online counseling, the skills required are similar to face-to-face counseling but need to be translated to a new medium. Rosenfield (2003: 98) describes one of the biggest advantages of telephone counseling to be the enabling of the client to take a fair measure of control over the session because they can hang up at any point, and therefore highlights the need for establishing a good contract and procedure in light of this. Telephone counseling is also more comfortable for the client in that it takes place in his or her own surroundings.

Honed listening skills can bring their own rewards within the therapy process. Without a facial or body reaction, the slightest pause or change in tone of voice can speak volumes with regard to what is happening for the client. Perceived anonymity mixed with the direct nature of speaking directly into another person's ear can create an intimacy which can invite strong fantasies of the other person, and transference issues. There is also an element of disinhibition with telephone work, which can speed up the therapeutic process but also alarm the client leading to early termination. As with other forms of distance counseling, ascertaining the reasons for seeking telephone counseling can be pertinent to the therapeutic work and should be sought.

MOBILE PHONES/SMS AS COMMUNICATION TOOLS

Use of a mobile or cell phone has been considered unsuitable for therapy in the past because of signal or battery failure, possible dangers while driving, and confidentiality (Payne et al., 2006). While these remain valid considerations, the improvement in mobile technologies means that signal and battery issues are less problematic, non hands-free mobile phone usage and driving has been made illegal in many countries or states in the case of the USA, and many people increasingly use mobile phones instead of a landline, meaning that as long as the environment is paid attention to, confidentiality remains the responsibility of the people in contact.

McEnery West and Mulvena (2008) consider the convenience of mobile phones in that they are a facility with one owner and with a private answer phone, missed calls are registered, and messages can be picked up instantly. In many ways this seems preferable to a landline and therapists may choose to have two devices with one specifically dedicated to client work. An advantage of this is that it is easier to explain to the client within the contracting stage exactly when it will be turned on or off, and when messages will be picked up. Therefore, while the client feels supported in having a dedicated line to the therapist, they are also able to be realistic in their expectations of when they may receive a response.

Texting, or SMS, is increasingly a convenient method of communication for arranging, reminding, or cancelling appointments. However, care should be taken of the client in assuming this is appropriate. Recent posts on a public forum from a client commented on how she 'felt quite let down' and 'hurt' that the therapist had cancelled their appointment by text message. Conversely, where provision of a therapist's mobile phone number can be extremely convenient, it also brings with it the opportunity for clients to text, often without consideration of any possible breach of boundaries or contracts. Ongoing support, in light of the perceived availability of the therapist, can easily be demanded, seeming quite natural to the client for whom texting is second nature. Indeed, this has been invited by some therapists for whom client safety is of immediate concern, and anecdotally has saved lives within the context of a student counseling service (Brice, 1999).

In addition to this, the use of texting to conduct actual therapeutic conversations is becoming increasingly apparent. Because of the instant nature of texting, care must be taken as to whom texts are being sent to, just as is the case with email. Moreover, the truncated nature of texts invites examination of our own interpretations of what message is being received, rather than paying attention to a possibly different intention from the client simply because they may have a different (possibly better) understanding of the use of texts in their culture. For example, Walker (2004) indicated her surprise when a client terminated a 2-year plus face-to-face relationship via a text message.

The instant and sometimes rash use of texts by the therapist can result in serious ramifications if used within an unboundaried relationship or one that is failing to maintain the therapeutic framework in which clearly ethical, and therefore safe, behavior thrives. In 2009, a therapist's use of texts (among other behaviors) such as, 'I'm here 4 u, always, deepest luv affection' and 'lots of warm fuzzy's 4 u to guide threw the darkest moments. Now 4 ever', resulted in removal of membership from the BACP. Even innocuous texts intended only to express caring can be intrusive, for example if sent on Christmas Day, New Years Day or at 3am in the morning. Text messages, including the dates and times they are sent, are a verbatim account of conversations just as much as email or chat logs are, and could be produced in courts or tribunals easily.

Cooper (2008) cites a case that actually includes SMS texting within a face-to-face session. A therapist who was in-session with a teenage female client with mobile in hand and texting could sense the client's frustration, when suddenly the therapist's own cell phone indicated a new text message had arrived. The client advised the therapist to check the message, as the client had texted 'u r not getting what Im saying'. The therapist stated that she has become more tolerant of such use of technology within sessions because SMS texting is part of the adolescent and youth or young adult culture. There is therefore an argument for the use of the therapist's mobile phone to be kept on when working with certain client groups.

MOBILE PHONES AS APPLICATION DELIVERY

A secondary way of considering the use of mobile phones is their ability to be used as platforms for software applications to be delivered to. Increasingly, online services such as My Mobile Guru (voice recordings on various mental health topics such as health, sex and relationships) are being designed to be delivered to mobile devices at a cost (www.mymobileguru.co.uk). These types of applications (apps) are only an electronic version of a leaflet (Hodson quoted in Roberts, 2008). Developments in Japan include websites delivered to mobiles where the user can input answers to cognitive questions and receive a diagnosis before being directed to similar documents on mental health topics. The concept of a 'Doctor in your pocket' was convincingly explored in a 2009 report from GSMA (Ivatury et al., 2009) drawing on examples from developing countries (suggesting that Western nations have much to learn from them regarding eHealth), and the UN and Vodafone released a study detailing 51 programs in 26 countries, with the biggest adopters being India (11 projects) and South Africa and Uganda (with six each) (Vital Wave Consulting, 2009).

Anger Diary, is a mood diary developed by a senior clinical psychologist who became interested in the potential of using mobile applications because, while using paper anger diaries when working with young people on anger control, she found low compliance:

> In my clinical experience with Anger Management over 20 years now I have found it almost impossible to get Anger Diaries recorded by clients out of session ... Most often there is very poor compliance so we end up completing retrospective diaries which are less accurate. (Personal communication)

She thought it would be worth exploring if adolescent clients would be more willing to complete an anger diary on their mobile phones, using the existing paper template for recording anger events which the mobile anger diary followed, such as date, time and location of the event, who was there, what was happening before, and thoughts and emotions around it.

In order to provide clients with privacy, the mobile diary was designed to be inconspicuous. If peers were to look at the client's phone they would have no idea what the program was for, as it was labelled simply 'AD'. It has no other identifying information and no graphical icon. Furthermore, a 4-digit code prevents anyone from opening the program up. It is also possible for clients to record anger events online, in and outside therapeutic sessions. SMS reminders were essential to the success of the anger management program.

VOIP

Voice over Internet Protocol (see Wikipedia, 2009a for more information) is a general term for various communication technologies that are delivered over the Internet. With perhaps the best known in this context being Skype, calls to other users online are free and in addition, it is designed to be part of a transparent communications system in that it is compatible for landlines (although usually for a charge). Video and text options are often bundled into software such as Skype, and everything is encrypted. As broadband improves, many organizations are finding it cheaper to switch to this way of communication, and this seems likely to spread further into personal use. It is the authors' opinion, however, that while VoIP will be useful in therapy in the future, current bandwidth between therapist and client is insufficient to provide an effective platform for conducting a therapeutic relationship.

PODCASTING

Podcasting became popular in around 2005 and is a technology that allows audio and video content via the Internet, which can also be stored on PCs and MP3 players and portable digital devices such as iPods. The process of creating a podcast is relatively cheap and is an effective way of broadcasting to a large number of people, hence its uptake by the profession for disseminating mental health information and advice. Quinones (in press) cites anecdotally the positive emails he has received from 'podcast clients' who benefit from using the information in a podcast to help themselves. Many of his podcast clients do not have or have limited access to professional mental health resources, in locations such as India or Iraq. However, there are also many cultural issues inherent in the global nature of podcasting, and what may be used for self-help in one community could be very offensive in another. In the future, Apple TVs – a box that can stream vast numbers of audio and video podcasts – may well be a feature in health care settings for clients as an option for receiving help and information on mental health issues.

WEBSITES AND WIKIS

Mental health websites will be very familiar to the reader. These collections of static web pages will usually contain at least a definition of a condition, its symptoms, treatments, resources and links to other information. A single person usually authors and edits each website, which is what distinguishes them from being a wiki. The abundance of mental health websites is likely to grow even more as the Internet finds its feet in its new incarnations (see Web 2.0 below).

Wikis differ from websites in that anyone can edit them or add new information, and this process is kept verbatim – including discussions (and often arguments) over what is being added or edited. Wikipedia is probably the best known wiki in that it is an open-edit encyclopaedia, but they are also used by organizations to bring a large project together with all the details of its development through collaboration. However, the use of the wiki in mental health is yet to fully realize its potential by large national professional organizations who may feel threatened by the possibility of the open editing process meaning a lack of control over content, although technically this can be 'closed down' to a select group of people. Wikis allow for a constantly updating set of resources for an international audience, and a wiki is particularly relevant for a field based on technology because of its ever changing face. Professionals familiar with mental health, technology and cyberspace are embracing wikis as the way forward for sharing and disseminating information, as can be seen from the work of ISMHO (members only at the time of writing), and the Online Therapy Institute (open to all) (Anthony and Nagel, 2009). The trace of edits and discussions may also prove invaluable in the event of malicious edits taking place – either by posting erroneous material or editing out acceptable material. Advising clients to use wikis as a source of mental health research should always be tinged with advice on the nature of wikis in general and the reliability of their content. Grohol (in press), however, points out that at the moment, because clients are more likely to come across blogs or websites before they find a wiki for information, 'their potential for harm is probably the least'.

VIDEOCONFERENCING

Despite the seemingly obvious benefits of videoconferencing for therapy over text-based therapy in that it may be seen as being nearer to face-to-face exchanges, the take-up of private communication has been slower than may have been predicted. This is in part due to the difficulty in achieving 'adequate results with consumer-level technology' (Holmes and Ainsworth, 2004: 261). It has, however, been keenly taken up by those who live in remote areas worldwide or those whose freedom is somehow impaired by a prison sentence or being housebound. Simpson (in press) points out that at some point in the future it may be considered unethical to withhold videotherapy for these communities in particular. As with other technologies and the ethical framework identified in Chapter 4, Koocher (2007) restates the importance of encryption and other security measures being in place.

Rees and Stone (2005) studied the rating of the therapeutic alliance in a face-to-face session against one conducted by video, and found a significant difference in the ratings, with video being much lower. This indicates that professionals remain suspicious of videoconferencing, since the content of the video and face-to-face sessions was identical. However, an early study (Simpson et al., 2001) reported that 90 percent of clients themselves expressed satisfaction with the service and some actually preferred it to face-to-face therapy. Although it may be seen as simply an electronic means of conducting or replicating face-to-face therapy, reported benefits to clients involve valuing the privacy, anonymity and lack of intimidation with video therapy (Bakke et al., 2001). A comprehensive overview of video counseling and psychotherapy in practice has been produced by Simpson (2003).

BLOGS

The personal journal as a therapeutic tool has been around for a long time (Thompson, 2004), but has rarely been in the public domain with the facility for feedback to be given to the blogger by the world at large. As with other uses of technology in counseling and psychotherapy, we are already behind in forming a coherent research base from which to make informed opinion about the implications of such phenomena (Anthony, 2004). Anthony also suggests 'practitioners, particularly online practitioners (whose clients are more likely to accept Internet communication as a viable alternative to face-to-face communication) have some measure in place when contracting with their client about the boundaries of acceptable spaces where the therapy or therapist are discussed' (Anthony, 2004: 38). This is something that is now more established and adopted by organizations such as the BACP, and increasingly professionals are being asked to speak and consult on this topic, alongside professional uses of networking sites and other newer elements of cyberspace.

The therapist may also want to establish boundaries within the therapeutic relationship *about* a client's personal blog (Thompson, 2008). Some clients may announce that they have a blog in the hope that the therapist will read the blog regularly. Other therapists may come across a blog that a client has written. Establishing boundaries around these issues during the informed consent process can be essential in the case of the client having a personal blog, particularly if it is about their mental wellbeing.

From the client's point of view, it must be noted that a person blogs in response to thought, action, or occurrence, and then posts the blog to the Internet within minutes. Similarly, comments may be posted onto the blog with a quick and affective response. In either case, the blogger or the person leaving a comment has no control over when any response may be read. Blogging as a form of self-therapy may provide symptomatic relief, self-reflection, and an opportunity to develop one's own voice (Tan, 2008). While this type of immediate cathartic release may be similar to placing words on the pages of a private journal, the aftermath that follows the use of blogging as journaling may be experienced much differently, particularly in light of disinhibition online. Emotionally charged entries related to the blogger's personal history might result in an immediate feeling of relief and initially increase a person's ego strength but when the blogger realizes that others have or will read the entry, the blogger may feel vulnerable and exposed (Nagel and Anthony, 2009). Depending on whether the blogger revealed events experienced as traumatic, the permanency of the blog and the others' ability to leave comments may actually trigger a re-traumatizing response. Therapist knowledge of these issues means they have the information to hand to be able to assist the client therapeutically in light of such responses to technological tools.

COMPUTERIZED COGNITIVE-BEHAVIORAL THERAPY (CCBT) AND COMPUTER-AIDED PSYCHOTHERAPY (CP)

While it has been argued that CCBT may be little more than an electronic self-help book, there is no doubt about the usefulness of programs such as FearFighter and Beating The Blues, both of which were sanctioned by the National Institute of Clinical Excellence (NICE, 2006) in the UK in 2006, and which address anxiety and depression respectively. Both are now in use in the UK in the National Health Service and in private health care, by both practitioners and clients. These CCBT packages are developed by professionals and then delivered to the client via the Internet, CD-ROM or telephone key-pad/voice response, usually via a ladder of modules (or sessions) which teach CBT techniques such as changing automatic thoughts, scheduling activities, problem solving, challenging core beliefs and similar. Modeling by other 'clients' are played via video and/or audio, and the end of the program usually focuses on long-term goals and relapse prevention.

CCBT is a convenient method of CBT delivery, as it can be accessed from home via various routes. This avoids travel costs, of course, but – as with other forms of technology – there are also distinct reasons for clients having a preference for CCBT, in that there is a lack of personal interaction, less intensity (clients can take breaks), less stigma, and because it is as flexible as any asynchronous method of service delivery. Inputting text into a computer program is as affected by disinhibition as much as other technologies that do not rely on physically being in the same room as another human being. Marks et al. (2007) also note that even undertaking the course with another person watching does not affect disinhibition, as the computer is seen as being 'confidential' – therefore, in this context 'confidential' can mean 'I can't tell it face-to-face' rather than 'I don't want my clinician to know'.

Clients do need to be motivated to continue with CCBT programs, and this can be enhanced by the look and tone of the material being presented which can have personal settings to reflect the preferred gender, age, accent and so on. Motivation can also be gained by the ability of the user to generate and print progress charts over time, and these are additionally also easily fed into management reports and other organizational tools to improve service delivery and manage health care budgets.

Marks et al. (2007), in their extensive book on the topic, identify the main areas where computer-aided psychotherapy is of particular use:

- Phobia and panic disorder

  o Such as spider, dental-injection, flying, social phobia; delivered to PC, DVD, CD-ROM, handheld devices for homework, and the Internet

- Obsessive compulsive disorder

  o Delivered by palmtop and laptop, with brief phone support

- Post-traumatic stress disorder

  o Delivered via email support for cognitive restructuring

- General anxiety and emotional problems

  o Functions range from relaxation, enhancement of counseling and stress management

- Depression

  o Such as Beating The Blues

- Eating disorders

  o Delivered by handheld computers, CD-ROM and automated SMS texting

- Substance misuse

  o Such as smoking and alcohol intake; delivered by website, email, online peer support

- Physical pain and distress

  o Such as headaches, back pain, tinnitus, burn-pain; delivered by website sometimes with email and phone support

GAMING

Attempts at engaging children or adolescents to tell their story through direct dialogue can often come to a standstill. Whereas for adults, dialogue in traditional therapy is the favored means of communication, children and adolescents often struggle to express themselves with words alone. Gaming, whether online or using platforms such as those made by Sony or Nintendo, is a simulation and as such is a safe environment in which to experiment and most importantly, in which to fail. These games can be cathartic, allowing players to deal with and master sensitive and difficult situations. Games provide the therapists with a way into the client's world. Matthews and colleagues at Trinity College Dublin in Ireland developed a game called Personal Investigator, which is best described in their own terms:

> Personal Investigator (PI) is a 3D computer game designed to help engage adolescents in psychotherapy. The game targets adolescents with mental health problems such as depression, anxiety and social skills problems. It was intended firstly as a computer-mediated tool to aid therapeutic conversations between adolescents and therapists and secondly for potential self-directed use online. PI employs a 'detective' narrative, but instead of playing the role of a *private* investigator, the teenager plays the role of a *personal* investigator hunting for solutions to personal problems. The choice of a 3D environment allows the young person the potential to pace and personalize their journey through the game. The aim is to create an engaging fantasy environment and empower adolescents to direct their own therapy. In collaboration with the therapist, the game aims to help clients to set their own therapeutic goals, recognize their own strengths and values, identify people in their lives who can support them, teach new coping strategies and focus on their future not their past. The game serves to break this therapeutic process

into a series of structured goals, which the adolescent can understand and achieve more easily. (Matthews et al., 2006: 31)

Such games are in development for use on mobile platforms to allow the gamer to work on the therapeutic material wherever and whenever he or she chooses. Pilot research on the use of 3D games for therapeutic use indicate that both therapist and client enjoy them and find them beneficial, and for the therapist, that they integrate well with traditional approaches (Coyle et al., 2005). In addition, development of the game has led to development of the software behind the scenes, allowing the therapist to tailor the game software to each client's own circumstances or presenting problems.

AVATARS AND VIRTUAL REALITY ENVIRONMENTS

Avatars (a graphical representation of a human being in a computer graphical environment) and virtual reality is currently seeing an explosion in popularity, as bandwidths increase and software becomes more and more developed. In 2002, Goss and Anthony wrote:

> Whether 'avatar therapy' is to become one element of the future of counselling and psychotherapy is yet to be seen. But given the pace of developments in the field it is impossible to rule it out and those practitioners with a technological bent might do well to keep an eye open for whatever uses it may, ultimately, be shown to have. What other innovations the technologists might have up their virtual sleeves we will have to wait and see. (Goss and Anthony, 2002: 15)

Avatar therapy is now a part of the 'the future' discussed then, with therapy taking place in the Massively Multiplayer Online (MMO) online platform Second Life (SL) (Wilson, in press). Daniel (2008) cites an online strategy analysis that predicts massive growth of up to one billion people taking part in a (non-gaming) virtual world by 2018. Second Life has its own currency, which begs fascinating analysis of what therapy costs in a virtual world in relation to the traditional fiscal system.

In SL at least, communication is made by typing on a keyboard (the avatar types onto air (an invisible keyboard) to indicate that the person is typing), and text appears above the avatar's head. Confidentiality is easily breached in this case because the text may be seen by anyone standing close enough to the conversation. This can be lessened by the use of a private secure 'skybox', a private environment that is accessible only to those invited. Further enhancement of security may include the use of an encrypted chat/VoIP platform such as Skype. The combination of a skybox and the use of encrypted text and chat adds a secure form of communication.

Although VoIP is available, this changes the beauty of the pure virtually enhanced textual relationship, with all that goes with it, such as fantasy, transference, projection and disinhibition. All these are facilitated by the choice of avatar – essentially creating a fantasy figure of the self. Wilson (2008) anecdotally reports one client who often switches between two avatars for sessions, depending on his or her mood. Using an encrypted chat program in addition to the virtual platform may be cumbersome unless the client and therapist have the aid of two computer screens or can utilize a split screen. A therapist may choose instead to meet the client in the virtual world in order to experience the client's virtual representation through an avatar and then process the meeting via encrypted chat or email (Valeeva, 2009).

What is fascinating about virtual reality is the endless opportunities it offers, limited only by imagination (see Wright and Anthony, 2003, for example) and possibly budgets. Virtual Reality Therapy is not new and the use of avatars need not always be involved, because other physical sensations can be replicated through the use of head-sets (visual and auditory simulation), vibrating floors or chairs (physical simulation), data gloves (touch simulation) and smells. Virtual environments are extremely flexible and as a result can be tailored to the needs of the client(s). It is not necessary for the client to receive therapy in a room that looks like a traditional therapy room. The client could be offered a venue that best facilitates the discussion or choose from a range of available rooms (Anthony and Lawson, 2002).

With the increasing sophistication of technology and the ability to turn virtual platforms into landscapes that are as real as looking out of a window, more and more therapeutic uses of avatar therapy can be considered. Various eclectic techniques and modalities can be incorporated into the therapy with three-dimensional components. Melding together many existing concepts into one fluid process online is already within reach. The use of avatars in therapy provides the ability to look at oneself objectively and rationally, as Suler says:

> The basic assumption of avatar psychotherapy is that all of the personae created in the virtual scenario are the various manifestations of the client's psyche. Those avatars concretize the complex constellations of memories, fears, wishes, idealizations, and expectations that comprise the client's sense of self. Those avatars give clients the opportunity to amplify, explore, modify, and develop those sectors of self. (1999: para. 15)

The use of avatar therapy can be very useful in dealing with childhood trauma, abusive relationships and grief and loss scenarios. Avatar therapy can also be helpful in assisting a client to create a new vision in life or a new ending to an existing situation. Countless stories can be enacted in a virtual world platform depending on the sophistication of the software.

But caution should be exercised when using the power of such virtual worlds and avatars to assist people in healing, especially if the virtual world is augmented to include material from the client's past or envisioned future. We can already be re-traumatized by the posting of old photos by other people in social environments where we were not expecting them to appear. In therapies such as this, careful preparation should be taken with the client to ensure safety and containment. For instance, if the client discloses personal information too quickly or if material that is significant to the client is used as explorative or to re-enact, the client can be re-traumatized when earlier trauma memories emerge. Therapists are advised to seek training in various trauma theories as well as in the use of technology to deliver avatar therapies. Therapists trained properly will understand the importance of pacing and timing in therapy, to allow the client's story to flow safely and without debilitating consequences. The therapist has the responsibility of modulating the emotional intensity throughout the process (Holloway, 2009).

Including other helpful tools such as collage boards allows the client to insert therapeutic material that he or she may find important in the journey even if they are not fully conscious about why a particular picture or word is important. For instance, embarking on therapy in a virtual world that offers sophisticated capabilities such as rapid development of avatars and surroundings from pictures, or sound infusion with previously selected music or voices, could involve an initial client intake that is much more in-depth than we normally consider. The therapy has a 3D quality, therefore the initial intake might involve the same.

Along with the standard list of questions provided on a questionnaire, the client might be asked to create a visual and/or audio collage of pictures and sounds that appeal to the client, have some meaning (known or unknown) to the client, or represent previous life experiences. In this way, the client is given the opportunity ahead of time to choose what items may be pulled from the collage to enhance the therapeutic story. Since the client has been well prepared and has chosen the material, the therapist has a better opportunity of titrating or modulating emotions that may arise during therapy. Even for the client who is not necessarily entering therapy with the idea of utilizing recreations or new creations, it is wise for the trained therapist to conduct a thorough, three-dimensional intake and assessment so that if therapy produces an opportunity for the client, much of the visual and auditory triggers have been gathered already. Of course, during the course of therapy the client could decide at any time to add (or remove) material to (or from) the collage board.

SOCIAL AND PROFESSIONAL NETWORKS

The arrival of the many social – and now professional – networks online has led to a rise in unexpected ethical dilemmas for therapists, and is now covered in both the BACP Guidelines (Anthony and Goss, 2009) and in the Online Therapy Institute Ethical Framework for being an online professional. Websites such as Facebook, Twitter and the upsurge of Ning sites all extend our communication with friends, family, colleagues and complete strangers to potentially a 24 hour a day occupation, particularly for those who take advantage of mobile or cell phone delivery. Updates of our every move can be sent, and it is only a matter of time before clients do not find it abnormal to send tweets (short <140 character messages) from therapy: 'If docs are now twittering from surgery, could twittering from one's therapy session be far behind? "Just told therapist I hate my parents"' (Grohol, 2009a). Grohol (2009b: para 9) also points out that 'We simply know how to talk, and Twitter is the first text service to adequately mimic this behavior in an online medium.'

Facebook and similar sites allow for the development of applications, starting with rating how similar tastes are with contacts, for example for films and books. However, recent developments also include apps for rating one's level of depression (Grohol, 2008, after

Goldberg, 1993) where scores can be automatically listed on one's homepage, although this is an optional feature. It should be noted that there is considerable debate surrounding the use of routine screening tests for mental illnesses, including depression, which have been found to offer no benefits in terms of improving the numbers of people recognized to have the condition, and next to no change in the interventions received or the outcomes obtained (Gilbody et al., 2001). What is more, there are undoubted pitfalls in the use of routine screening measures (Coyne et al., 2001, 2000), especially when self-administered. Whether it is wise for such highly personal and possibly misunderstood diagnostic information to then be made publicly available to one's family, friends, acquaintances and professional colleagues, and possibly even clients, is a moot point.

Careful thought is needed about how we interact with each other on these platforms, and what pitfalls there are in an arena where dual relationships are possible such as a supervisor being a friend on Facebook, or a client witnessing tweets and 'following' them (and maybe therefore 'you'). Clients and colleagues can comment on pictures of what you were up to at the weekend, or your friends may get fed up with notifications of automated postings from Twitter regarding how your latest work project is going. Your relationship status is seen by everyone you are linked to, and notifications are sent out if this changes, inviting sometimes not very sympathetic or thought-through comments. All these points need consideration when you are an online professional, whether working with clients in that environment or not.

CONCLUDING THOUGHTS: WEB 2.0 AND BEYOND

As stated in the Introduction, 'The term "Web 2.0" describes the changing trends in the use of World Wide Web technology and web design that aim to enhance creativity, communications, secure information sharing, collaboration and functionality of the web' (Wikipedia, 2009b). The implications of this for the mental health field is unknown, although the discussions throughout this chaper invite many examples of Web 2.0 in action, particularly with regard to networking, blogging and wikis.

The creativity and collaboration of Web 2.0 invites a strong prediction that in the future, clients will be at least a part of planning the therapeutic process every bit as much as the practitioner is now, including the ethical framework of traditional therapies. Thus, a wiki can invite edits and discussion from the users of a service to enable the providers to change and develop a service to be the best fit and also best practice for their client group. A blog can invite comments to service change proposals, and online networks of clients can support or take down a particular service with a few carefully placed clicks on a five-star rating or thumbs-up/thumbs-down facility.

Web 2.0 offers equal power to us all – clients and practitioners alike. The collaboration of service providers and end-users will evolve into a free-flowing, flexible arrangement where the 'expert' is considered to be anyone. It is the client who makes the therapy work, not the therapist. We already have evidence of this as clients use blogs to 'self-therap' as they used to use journals, as they use the convenience of electronic facilities to connect with other human beings where they used to write letters, and as they find information online to tell their doctor or physician how to treat their ailments where they used to accept a prescription, to name but a few applications.

The use of technology in everyday life is already second nature to the potential clients and professionals of the future. The profession of therapy and mental health needs not only to recognize this, but be ready to accept and embrace the concept of Web 2.0 and any incarnation of the Internet that follows. The traditional and central facets of counseling and psychotherapy as we understand them need to be woven into our work and society on a daily basis, rather than for 50 minutes once a week, for example. In the past, technology seems to have led the profession – sometimes grudgingly – into accepting the presence of it within therapeutic service provision. Now, by embracing Web 2.0, we – as practitioners, the profession, and clients – can be who we want to be.

REFERENCES

Anthony, K. (2004) 'The Art of Blogging', in *BACP Counselling and Psychotherapy Journal*, 15(9): 38.

Anthony, K. and Goss, S. (2009) *Guidelines for Online Counselling and Psychotherapy, 3rd edition*. Lutterworth: BACP.

Anthony, K. and Lawson, M. (2002) 'The Use of Innovative Avatar and Virtual Environment Technology for Counselling and Psychotherapy', in *KateAnthony.co.uk*. Unpublished paper. Available at www.kateanthony.co.uk/InnovativeAvatar.pdf [accessed 9 April 2009].

Anthony, K. and Nagel, D.M. (2009) 'Online Therapy Wiki', in *Online Therapy Institute*. Available at www.onlinetherapy.wikispaces.com [accessed 9 April 2009].

Bakke, B., Mitchell, J., Wonderlicht, S. and Erikson, R. (2001) 'Administering Cognitive Behavioural Therapy for Bulimia Nervosa via Telemedicine in Rural Settings', in *International Journal of Eating Disorders*, 30(4): 454–7.

Brice, A. (1999) Personal communication.

Cooper, G. (2008) 'Therapy and Global Warming', in *Psychotherapy Networker*. Available at www.psychotherapynetworker.org/online-courses/OL125?category=distance_learning& sub_cat=all_courses&type=online [accessed 9 April 2009].

Coyle, D., Matthews, M., Sharry, J., Nisbet, A. and Doherty, G. (2005) 'Personal Investigator: A Therapeutic 3D Game for Adolescent Psychotherapy', in *International Journal of Interactive Technology and Smart Education*, 2(2): 73–88.

Coyne, J.C., Palmer, S. and Thompson, R. (2001) 'Additional Pitfalls of Routine Screening', in *BMJ*. Available at www.bmj.com/cgi/eletters/322/7283/406#12774 [accessed 9 April 2009].

Coyne, J.C., Thompson, R., Palmer, S.C., Kagee, A. and Maunsell, E. (2000) 'Should we Screen for Depression? Caveats and Pitfalls', in *Applied and Preventative Psychology*, 9(2): 101–21.

Daniel, J. (2008) 'The Self Set Free', in *Therapy Today*, 19(9): 5.

Gilbody, S., House, A. and Sheldon, T. (2001) 'Routinely Administered Questionnaires for Depression and Anxiety: Systematic Review', in *BMJ*, 322(7283): 406–9.

Goss, S. and Anthony, K. (2002) 'Virtual Counsellors – Whatever Next?', in *BACP Counselling and Psychotherapy Journal*, 13(2): 14–15.

Goss, S. and Anthony, K. (eds) (2003) *Technology in Counselling and Psychotherapy: A Practitioner's Guide*. Basingstoke, UK: Palgrave.

Grohol, J. (2008) 'Depression Test', in *Facebook*. Available at http://apps.facebook.com/depressionquiz/take [accessed 9 April 2009].

Grohol, J. (2009a) Tweet sent 19/02/2009, replicated at Facebook [accessed 25 February 2009].

Grohol, J. (2009b) 'The Psychology of Twitter', in *PsychCentral*. Available at http://psychcentral.com/blog/archives/2009/02/23/the-psychology-of-twitter/ [accessed 9 April 2009].

Grohol, J. (in press) 'Websites, Blogs and Wikis in Mental Health', in K. Anthony and D.M. Nagel (eds), *Mental Health and the Impact of Technological Development*. Springfield, IL: Charles Thomas Publisher.

Holloway, D. (2009) 'Interview – DeeAnna Nagel and Kate Anthony, Online Therapy Institute', in *The Metaverse Journal*, 30 March. Available at http://www.metaversejournal.com/2009/03/30/interview-deeanna-nagel-and-kate-anthony-online-therapy-institute/ [accessed 9 April 2009].

Holmes, L. and Ainsworth, M. (2004) 'The Future of Online Counseling', in R. Kraus, J. Zack and G. Stricker (eds), *Online Counseling: A Handbook for Mental Health Professionals*. San Diego, CA.:Elsevier Academic Press.

Ivatury, G., Moore, J. and Bloch, A. (2009) *A Doctor in Your Pocket: Health Hotlines in Developing Countries*. London: GSMA Development Fund.

Koocher, G. (2007) 'Twenty-first Century Ethical Challenges for Psychology', in *American Psychologist*, 62(5): 375–84.

Logan, H. and Trench, K. (2007) 'Effective Telephone Counselling', presentation given to TalktoaCounsellor.co.uk, London, May.

Marks, I., Cavanagh, K. and Gega, L. (2007) *Hands-on Help: Computer Aided Psychotherapy*. New York: Psychology Press.

Matthews, M., Coyle, D. and Anthony, K. (2006) 'Personal Investigator', in *Therapy Today*, 17(7): 30–3.

Matthews, M., Doherty, G. and Delahunty, A. (2009) Anger Diary. Personal communication.

McEnery West, C. and Mulvena, T. (2008) 'Text Speak', in *Therapy Today*, 19(8): 21–8.

Nagel, D.M. and Anthony, K. (2009) 'Writing Therapy using New Technologies – the Art of Blogging', in *Journal of Poetry Therapy*, 22(1): 41–5.

NICE (2006) *Guidance on the Use of Computerised Cognitive Behavioural Therapy for Anxiety and Depression. Technology Appraisal no. 97*. London: National Institute for Clinical Excellence.

Payne, L., Casemore, R., Neat, P. and Chambers, M. (2006) *Guidelines for Telephone Counselling and Psychotherapy*. Rugby: BACP Publications.

Quinones, M. (in press) 'Podcasting in Mental Health', in K. Anthony and D.M. Nagel (eds), *Mental Health and the Impact of Technological Development*. Springfield, IL: Charles Thomas Publisher.

Rees, C. and Stone, S. (2005) 'Therapeutic Alliance in Face-to-Face versus Videoconferenced Psychotherapy', in *Professional Psychology: Research and Practice*, 36 (6): 649–53.

Roberts, D. (2008) 'Can Therapy on your Mobile Really Work?', in *Guardian.co.uk*. Available at www.guardian.co.uk/lifeandstyle/2008/sep/15/healthandwellbeing.psychology [accessed 9 April 2009].

Rosenfield, M. (2003) 'Telephone Counselling and Psychotherapy in Practice', in S. Goss and K. Anthony (eds), *Technology in Counselling and Psychotherapy: A Practitioner's Guide*. Basingstoke, UK: Palgrave.

Simpson, S. (2003) 'Video Counselling and Psychotherapy in Practice', in S. Goss and K. Anthony (eds), *Technology in Counselling and Psychotherapy: A Practitioner's Guide*. Basingstoke, UK: Palgrave.

Simpson, S. (in press) 'Videoconferencing in Mental Health', in K. Anthony and D.M. Nagel (eds), *Mental Health and the Impact of Technological Development*. Springfield, IL: Charles Thomas Publisher.

Simpson, S., Deans, G. and Brebner, E. (2001) 'The Delivery of a Tele-psychology Service to Shetland', in *Clinical Psychology and Psychotherapy*, 8(2): 130–5.

Suler, J. (1999) 'Avatar Psychotherapy', in *The Psychology of Cyberspace*. Available at http://www-usr.rider.edu/~suler/psycyber/avatarther.html [accessed 9 April 2009].

Tan, L. (2008) 'Psychotherapy 2.0: MySpace Blogging as Self-therapy', in *American Journal of Psychotherapy*, 62(2): 142–63.

THA (1999) *Guidelines for Good Practice*. London: Telephone Helplines Association. Available at www.helplines.org.uk [accessed 9 April 2009].

THA (2007) *Telephone Helplines in a Multi-Channel Environment*. London: Telephone Helplines Association.

Thompson, A. (2008) 'Counselor's Right to Privacy: Potential Boundary Crossings through Membership in Online Communities', in *Counseling Today*, 51(2): 44–5.

Thompson, K. (2004) 'Journal Writing as a Therapeutic Tool', in G. Bolton, S. Howlett, C. Lago and J. Wright, (eds), *Writing Cures*. Hove, UK: Brunner-Routledge.

Valeeva, A. (2009) 'Online Therapy Institute', in *InnerWorld Magazine*, 2 (March): 32–5.

Vital Wave Consulting (2009) *mHealth for Development. The Opportunity of Mobile Technology for Healthcare in the Developing World*. Washington, D.C. and Berkshire, UK: UN Foundation-Vodafone Foundation Partnership, 2009. Available at www.unfoundation.org/global-issues/technology/mhealth-report.html [accessed 9 April 2009].

Walker, S. (2004) 'To Text or Not to Text?', in *BACP Counselling and Psychotherapy Journal*, 15(3): 40.

Wikipedia (2009a) 'Voice over Internet Protocol', in *Wikipedia, The Free Encyclopedia*. Available at http://en.wikipedia.org/wiki/Voip [accessed 9 April 2009].

Wikipedia (2009b) 'Web 2.0', in *Wikipedia, The Free Encyclopedia*. Available at http://en.wikipedia.org/wiki/Web_2.0 [accessed 3 April 2009].

Wilson, J. (in press) 'Virtual Reality Environments in Mental Health', in K. Anthony and D.M. Nagel (eds), *Mental Health and the Impact of Technological Development*. Springfield, IL: Charles Thomas Publisher.

Wilson, J. (2008) Personal Communication.

Wright, J. and Anthony, K. (2003) (eds) 'Information Technology: Future Therapy Stories', in *BACP Counselling and Psychotherapy Journal*, 14(9): 22–5.

INDEX

Supporting researchers for more than forty years

Research methods have always been at the core of SAGE's publishing. Sara Miller McCune founded SAGE in 1965 and soon after she published SAGE's first methods book, *Public Policy Evaluation*. A few years later, she launched the Quantitative Applications in the Social Sciences series – affectionately known as the 'little green books'.

Always at the forefront of developing and supporting new approaches in methods, SAGE published early groundbreaking texts and journals in the fields of qualitative methods and evaluation.

Today, more than forty years and two million little green books later, SAGE continues to push the boundaries with a growing list of more than 1,200 research methods books, journals, and reference works across the social, behavioral, and health sciences.

From qualitative, quantitative and mixed methods to evaluation, SAGE is the essential resource for academics and practitioners looking for the latest in methods by leading scholars.

www.sagepublications.com